Anonymous

Euthanasia

Or, Turf, Tent and Tomb

Anonymous

Euthanasia
Or, Turf, Tent and Tomb

ISBN/EAN: 9783744756037

Printed in Europe, USA, Canada, Australia, Japan

Cover: Foto ©ninafisch / pixelio.de

More available books at **www.hansebooks.com**

COLLECTION

OF

BRITISH AUTHORS

TAUCHNITZ EDITION.

VOL. 2905.

EUTHANASIA; OR, TURF, TENT AND TOMB.

IN ONE VOLUME.

"Come, gentle Death, the ebbe of care;
    The ebbe of care, the flood of life;
  The flood of life, the joyful fare;
    The joyful fare, the end of strife;
  The end of strife: that thing wish I:
    Wherefore come, Death, and let me die!"

SIR THOMAS WYATT.

EUTHANASIA

OR

TURF, TENT AND TOMB.

LEIPZIG
BERNHARD TAUCHNITZ
1893.

EUTHANASIA.

CHAPTER I.

"We made mistakes in youth, my lad,
But they will not outlive us;
The worst we did was none so bad,
The world may well forgive us."
RENNELL RODD.

"FIVE to one bar one! five to one bar one! eight to one bar two! any price some of these others!"

These are the sounds which rise in a discordant chorus from the pandemonium of Tattersall's enclosure at Ascot on a hot afternoon in June—now rising to the pitch of an almost unintelligible roar, then again dying away to a comparative lull, sufficient only to give a short rest to the hardened lungs of the perspiring occupants of the "Ring."

"What are they making favourite, O'Connor?" are the words addressed in the tone of indifference habitually assumed on these occasions, to one of the leading members of the profession by one of that well-dressed crowd that is mostly found close against the railings separating the sacred precincts of the Royal Enclosure from the narrow space in which the fielders are huddled together.

There was nothing about the speaker's outward appearance that would cause him to be singled out from amongst the group in which he was standing. Clear blue eyes that look you straight in the face; a healthy, sunburnt complexion: features, if not of an absolutely faultless mould, nevertheless straight cut, and emphatically those of a gentleman; an upright, somewhat soldierly bearing are not very uncommon characteristics.

"Silverstreak, my lord," is the answer in a fine Hibernian brogue that many years spent on this side of St. George's Channel have failed to wipe away; "they are all going for her—in fact, there is no money for any of the others whatever."

Needless to say the answer was fully expected by the person to whom it was addressed. He knew all too well that his nominal yearly income—whatever that might be—shrank into absolute insignificance compared to the stakes he stood to win—or lose— on the favourite in the race for which the saddling-bell was then being rung.

Nevertheless, not a muscle moves on his face when, taking out his betting-book, he says:

"I'll take fifteen hundred to eight about the favourite, if you will lay it; or"—after a slight pause —"I will take it twice."

After a little demurring, the bet is duly booked,

swelling the total of Lord George Mansfield's invest-
ments on Silverstreak—chestnut mare by Silvester
out of Camilla—to a figure which would have made
the late Marquis, who knew every cab-fare in London,
and looked upon the outstretched hand of a crossing-
sweeper as something akin to a personal offence, well-
nigh turn in his grave.

Anyone who has been through similar experiences
will readily believe that Lord George, until his
suspense was over, was in no frame of mind to
devote any of his time to responding with more
than a commonplace remark to the many greetings
he received as he strode rapidly through the enclosure in search of a point of vantage from which
to view the forthcoming race for the Hunt Cup.

The most enticing smiles that accompany the
stereotyped question, "Oh! do tell me, what do you
think is going to win?" elicit no more than the somewhat curt reply, "They all say the favourite will!"
and a noble duchess, requesting him to put thirty
shillings on Silverstreak for a place, is surprised to
see that so desirable a commission should fail to
make him retrace his steps in the direction of the
ring.

Once only does he stop; for, coming towards him
in faultless attire, carrying his sixty years with the
ease of a boy, still chuckling at the last high-flavoured
story he has just imparted to a vision of mauve *crêpe
de chine* walking by his side, comes Lord Devereux,
the owner of Silverstreak.

"Have you seen the Cup yet, Lord Devereux?"

are his opening words, for he knows too much of
the world to ask an owner the odious question, "Is
your horse going to win?"

"No, my dear fellow; I can't say I have. Hope
to see it on my dinner-table to-night, though. I
think if I were you I would have a bit on."

This is all Lord George wants to hear, and he is
hardly in the frame of mind to make allowance for
the sanguine nature which makes Lord Devereux
feel rather injured whenever a horse, carrying his
colours, is not in the first three.

And now a stir is noticeable even amongst the
crowd in the enclosure, that happy mixture of a
garden-party and a race-course. Hungry chaperons
are for one moment forgetting the all-important question as to whether anybody will take them to luncheon;
young girls, whose thoughts until then have been
monopolized with mental invectives against "that
wretch of a Madame Lodo," who sent home their
last frock as wide as a sack, are beginning to study
their race-cards, and, from the Royal stand glasses
are levelled towards the far end of the New Mile.

After a few trifling breakaways, the flag has
fallen to a level start. An almost unbroken line,
with the exception of one or two stragglers, presents
itself to the eye, gradually approaching the bottom
of the dip previous to commencing that ascent that
has seen so many hopes dashed to the ground. The
clatter of tongues has ceased, to give way to the
silence of suspense, almost appalling in its intensity.
They have crossed the road and are gradually ap-

proaching that long extended line formed by the
various stands. No trace of emotion is perceptible
in Lord George's face, and the hand that holds up
his glasses is moved by no tremor, though he knows
that in a very few seconds his fate will be decided.

The favourite has a good berth close to the rails;
he is breasting the hill resolutely, and his jockey
has, as yet, never moved on him.

"What is that in yellow?" a voice is suddenly
heard to say, not far from where our friend has
taken up his position, closely followed by a shriek
from the ring. "How much Barrister? The favourite
don't win for a hundred."

Alas, for the glorious uncertainty! The favourite
answers gamely to his jockey's call, and a fine race
home ensues. The lad, riding a rank outsider thus
dropped from the clouds, is far too flurried at the
idea of riding a finish against a veteran like his
antagonist on Silverstreak, even to think of picking
up his whip, or the result might have been different.
All that human skill can do is done to secure the
judge's verdict, but it is not to be.

Up goes the number of Barrister, winner by half-
a-length.

A deadly pallor creeps over the face of the man
who knows his fate is now sealed; but not a syllable
escapes him. To him that number means poverty;
exile, at least, for many years to come; destruction
of all his hopes—nothing, in fact, before him but an
absolute blank.

"I hope you have not had a bad race, Lord

George—have you? Do come and let us have some luncheon!" These are the first words that meet his ear.

The speaker may well be considered worthy of more than a passing glance. The name of Mrs. John Arthur is as familiar to every reader of the *Universe, Veracity,* or other suppliers to the popular craving for society news as that of Wellington to the student of the Peninsular campaign.

In the social regions in which she holds sway, not to know "Mrs. Jack" would indeed be to argue oneself unknown.

The doors of her town house, a "desirable family mansion," situated in the very heart of what, amongst her set, is known as the "hot corner," are open at almost every hour of the twenty-four to her habitués, but to few others. Married without affection, and almost without the pretence of any, to a wealthy member of the Stock Exchange, whatever illusions she might have had speedily vanished. Her surprise would probably have been great had it ever dawned upon her that many might consider hers an empty, shallow, contemptible life. Any remarks which during her Sunday devotions she might occasionally hear from the pulpit on the wickedness of the pomps and vanities of this world, it would never have occurred to her to apply to herself; and had she ever caught herself inquiring into her inner life, she would probably have come to the conclusion that her liver was out of order, and that she required a cure at Carlsbad.

Blest with a splendid constitution, a quick intelligence, coupled with an early acquired knowledge of the world, her life had hardly been troubled with any other cares than the apprehension of her husband "doing something silly" on the Stock Exchange, or of getting herself talked about more than the social code of morality—the only one she stood in awe of—would tolerate. So, far, she had been fairly successful in the latter respect; for, though sailing dangerously close to the wind on more than one occasion, she had just managed to avoid bringing upon herself the frowns of that strangely-constituted Court of Justice that sits in judgment upon social offenders. True, its sternest verdict cannot go beyond ostracism from a certain fraction of what terms itself Society; and yet the holy dread of that verdict, coupled with remote visions of Sir J. Hannen, or, rather, Sir Francis Jeune, appearing as the avenger, are the only checks upon natures in which the curse of social ambition and conventionalism has stifled all notion of a nobler code of ethics.

That the class to whom these remarks apply is still a small one in the ocean of London society few would deny, fewer still that it is a rapidly-increasing one. No statistics are kept of the annual holocausts of feminine pride, honour and self-respect which are made to obtain admission into the charmed circle of what is termed a "smart set," with all the delightful privileges which intimacy with its leading members entails. Only a minute study of the deepest recesses of a woman's heart, from which she will do her very

utmost to ward the indiscreet gazes, even of those
for whom she has otherwise few secrets, will disclose
the intensity of delight felt at the safe accomplishment of every successive rung of the social ladder,
a satisfaction mostly shared, to some extent, by an
admiring, though somewhat bewildered, husband.

To a nature thus constituted, no work of art,
not the most glorious landscape upon which the
human eye ever feasted, nay, not even the most
passionate words that love can inspire, will evoke
anything approaching the gratification felt at being
able casually to repeat to a friend of humbler station
—formerly her equal—any remark addressed to her
at the Duchess of Birmingham's last little dance by
an illustrious personage.

To some, this picture may seem overdrawn. Let
those who think so examine more closely even their
own circle of acquaintances; let them ask any hostess
in London to produce the notes she has received a
fortnight before she gave her last ball, and let them
then accuse the writer of exaggeration.

"Nothing I should like better, Mrs. Jack; let us
try the Guards' tent. Yes, I did back the favourite,
the same as everybody else;" and he leads the way
across the course into that scene of lavish hospitality
with which the Household Brigade seem anxious to
return tenfold the civilities bestowed upon them during a London season.

Somewhat below the average height, with a waist
not exceeding eighteen inches, Mrs. Jack cannot be
described by her most ardent admirers as more than

an "awfully pretty little woman." The epithet of lovely would seem strangely out of place, if applied to what a Frenchman would describe as a *"petit minois chiffonné,"* with eyes remarkable more for their restlessness and quickness of perception than for anything else. Strength of will—possibly of passion (a bold man is he, or a very inexperienced one, who professes to form an opinion thereon from the outline of a woman's face)—is clearly depicted in the shape of the mouth, which, though generally, lending itself to a conventional smile, has a singularly set expression when at rest. The adjective with which to describe the colour of her hair might take some difficulty in finding, its hue being described once by an irreverent observer as reminding him of the oranges that grow around the terraces of Sorrento.

The Guards' tent, with a hungry multitude fighting for admission to the tables laden with every sort of delicacy to tempt the inner man, is a *milieu* ill-adapted for more than the most conventional of intercourse, though conventionalism in her conversation is not one of Mrs. Jack's besetting sins, and a man must indeed be slow of wit not soon to leave the range of platitudes when talking to her. She was once heard to exclaim:

"As long as a man does not say, 'What a fine day it is!' or, 'How lovely the Duchess of L.—— is looking!' he is all right, and I can get on with him."

She has the courage of her opinion in admitting

to a total want of interest in racing, and her question: "Have you got anything on this next race?" having been answered in the negative, they are left for the time in comparative solitude, once the bell has rung for the race following the Hunt Cup.

"I am sure you have lost a lot of money, have not you? You might tell me, at least," she says, with a sympathising glance, the expression of all others in a woman's eyes which finds the weak spot in every man's armour.

Few men care to talk much about themselves or their own affairs, though there are, no doubt, some striking and rather painful exceptions; nevertheless, the reticence which, at the best of times, is but acquired and artificial, may, when a real crisis in life is reached, make place for the moment to a deep craving for sympathy. Then, at least, what the Germans call *das rein Menschliche* comes to the front and sweeps away the hollow fabric of conventionalism.

"Do you really care to hear?" he answered. "Yes, I have had a bad race—so bad that my papers will have to go up before the end of the week, and the sooner I return to town and book a birth for Kimberley or G—d knows where, the better it will be for everybody. Of course you must have known for some time back that my affairs were in more of a muddle than usual. How can anyone live on that miserable pittance Errington allows me? As long as all his hospitals are flourishing I might starve for all he cared. I thought I would get home over this race and have a bit in hand, too; we know the result now."

Mrs. Arthur has never taken her eyes off him whilst he spoke, and there is a look of genuine sympathy in her face: she is capable of kind thoughts and even kind actions when her own private interests are not at stake.

"And how about Mildred Charteris?" she answers. Has she any idea of this state of things? And I suppose your engagement will have to be broken off now, won't it? I can't tell you how sorry I am for you!"

"Poor child! it is for her sake that I feel it most; and I don't know how I shall ever raise the courage to tell her. You know she isn't like you or me, or what in that long sermon the other day they called the worldlings. She is a *soul*—I don't mean one of the professional souls, but a real genuine one. Money matters don't exist for her; I told her I had a big bet on the Hunt Cup and that my affairs were not progressing satisfactorily, but she never even asked me what I had backed. Wasn't that funny?"

"No, not at all. I think it particularly nice of her, although you kindly remark she is so totally unlike me. But, do tell me, how long have you been engaged? Did you not propose to her when you were both children? I always thought there was some sort of romance about it, but as a rule you are so very reticent about your affairs."

"Well, there is not much to tell," he answered,

after a second's hesitation; "she lived with her old aunt, close to the Priory; we were perpetually thrown together as children, and in all my little troubles I would come to her as I would to a sister if I had one. One day—I was at Eton—when I came home for the holidays, I told her I had fallen in love with a girl down there (as a matter of fact it was the sister of the barmaid at Surley's), and poor Mildred burst into tears and sobbed her heart out. Next day I thought the matter over, and I went up to town and bought her a ring for thirty-five shillings, with a turquoise in it, and I told her I loved her the better of the two and she must one day be my wife. She is only a few years younger than I am, you know, and somehow she did not look a bit surprised; she only caught hold of my hand and said she would entrust me with her life's happiness. We have been obliged to keep it dark up to now on account of Errington, who cannot make up his mind whether he is going to do anything for us or not."

"I never heard quite such a pathetic story; it is a pity she did not keep you in better order once you were engaged. Did you go in for flirting too, or did you save all your energy for betting and gambling?"

"Of course I never flirted. Surely you have seen enough of me to know *that:* besides, the only woman with whom I might possibly have forgotten myself sufficiently to do such a thing never gave me a chance."

"And who might she be?"

"Don't you pretend not to know," he retorts, in

a tone of cheerful banter, his naturally good spirits rapidly rising again; "but it's no good thinking of all that as long as old Jim is to the front. Good old Jim, I wish I were in his shoes," he adds laughingly.

"Do you?" she replies pensively; "I don't, but your remarks are getting exceedingly frivolous; I think I shall have to tell Miss Charteris. Oh, but here she is!"

She rises to greet the young girl who, closely followed by Lord Devereux, is making her way into the tent. The latter is too much elated at the prospect of a long, undisturbed conversation with the young lady on whom he has set his elderly heart to fret about his recent defeat, and he accosts Lord George in his usual tone of careless good humour.

"So sorry, my dear fellow, I told you to back Silverstreak. Of course, after his running at Leicester, we never troubled any more about Barrister—warm lot in that stable, aren't they? What will you take, Miss Charteris?"

The habitually rather cold and distant expression upon the latter's countenance has become slightly more marked. Too young to be altogether free from self-consciousness, the notion is intensely distateful to her that Mrs. Jack Arthur might suspect her of having purposely followed Lord George; so she merely answers her veteran admirer's question by suggesting, under the pretence of more air, their sitting at a table on the farther side of the tent.

As he pours out a glass of champagne cup to the tall, dark girl by his side, Lord Devereux allows

his glance to rest, with a delightful sense of com-
placency and expectant proprietorship, upon the delicate outline of her features. Though he searches
in vain for any encouragement in those lustrous dark
eyes, of Oriental beauty, which seem to notice neither
him nor any of the tempting dishes he is handing to
her one after another, Lord Devereux is not to be discouraged, and is more than ever determind "to make
the running," as he would himself have expressed it.

He had led the conversation on to a marriage
recently announced, the parties to which could hardly
boast of a joint budget of eight hundred a-year.

"Believe me, Miss Charteris (I speak to you almost like a father; for, of course, I am old enough
to be your father over and over again), that sort of
thing never answers: you cannot live on bread and
cheese and kisses." His neighbour slightly winced,
but this was entirely lost upon him. "It's all very
well for the first six months. After that, when you
find you cannot join your friends' little play-parties
because Lacon and Ollier have written to say, "The
favour of a cheque is earnestly requested," and your
husband has got to stint himself in his after-dinner
claret, your evenings by the fireside will soon get to
pall upon both of you—mark my words, upon both
—before the first year is over."

"I suppose you are right, Lord Devereux," the
girl answered in rather a dreamy, absent manner;
"you must know a great deal more about it than I
do. I cannot say these are exactly my views, but I
don't feel as if I could make a single remark on the

subject that had not been made many thousands of times before in every intelligible language. Besides, as there is not much probability of my marrying anybody, rich or poor, for some time to come, it cannot matter much to anyone what I think on the subject, can it? Shall we go back to the other side now? What do you think?"

With a look of genuine disappointment upon his face, Lord Devereux empties his glass and escorts his fair charge back to the enclosure.

Once there, she has not many seconds to wait before she sees the stalwart form of Lord George approaching her. There is a heavy cloud on the young man's face that seems to confirm all her worst forebodings.

They drift apart from the group amongst which she had been standing. "Mildred, I have been so anxious to speak to you," are his opening words; "I have been most unlucky over the Hunt Cup; I am afraid it really is very serious indeed. It is no good attempting to talk the matter over in this bear-garden; might I come and see you to-morrow morning before racing? I am not at all sure of staying on to the end of the week."

She raises her eyes with a look of intense tenderness and compassion. "Yes, you will find me somewhere near the tennis-court any time after breakfast to-morrow. I am so very sorry;" and she holds out her hand to him. He grasps it, and uttering, with rather a hoarse voice, the one word, "Good-bye," he takes leave of her.

CHAPTER II.

"We look before and after,
    And pine for what is not:
    Our sincerest laughter
    With some pain is fraught;
Our sweetest songs are those that tell of saddest thought."
                                                SHELLEY.

THE races are pretty nearly over; an eager crowd is collecting to see the royal procession drive off; people are looking for their belongings, most of them feeling somewhat relieved at a long day being brought to a close.

Lord George is staying in the same party with Mrs. Jack Arthur, and they soon find themselves seated behind a showy team of bays and roans with which their host is driving them back to The Elms.

Whatever the results of the day may have been, as chronicled by the betting-book, there are probably few more delightful sensations than the return from the noise, bustle and excitement of Ascot Heath, to one of those many charming houses that surround it within a radius of some five or six miles. The knowledge that, for better, for worse, the struggle of the day is over; that flannels can take the place of frock-coats, and friendly intercourse that of a promiscuous exchange of commonplace remarks, gives a most refreshing feeling of relaxation to the weary mind and body.

Perhaps on these occasions our insular prejudice against "doing nothing" is carried somewhat too far. Anyhow, no one will be surprised that before The Elms are reached, Mrs. John Arthur should have suggested to her neighbour a quiet ride round Virginia Water to fill up the time before dinner. Needless to say, the invitation is eagerly accepted. In Lord George's present frame of mind some kind of excitement is indispensable; and after a short delay he finds himself by the side of a very smartly-turned-out little lady with a sailor hat most becomingly perched on her well-shaped head, handling a nicely-bred pony with showy action to the utmost perfection.

Very few minutes' ride bring them to the gates of Windsor Park, and they follow the path skirting Virginia Water. The rhododendrons are in full bloom; the rays of the setting sun are warded off by the luxuriant verdure overhead; not a sound is to be heard, and hardly a leaf is stirring.

They ride silently beside each other for a time. At last Mrs. Arthur, dropping her reins on the pony's neck, exclaims: "Isn't this heavenly—this intense solitude after all the noise and bustle? We might fancy ourselves a hundred miles from any human habitation. But it is not to make these general reflections that I have come out; for this evening we may not have a chance of talking. Tell me, what do you suppose will be your next move?"

She has really been thinking the matter over, and is working herself up into a genuine interest in her companion's fate.

"Do you think you might tide matters over just for the present? I daresay Jack might get you some berth in the City—*that* would be better than nothing. I don't want you to go round the world, or goodness knows where; I hate losing my friends, and we have been very good friends, haven't we?"

"Friends? Yes, I should think so, and we will always remain so, no matter where I am and whatever happens. I shall never forget the interest you have shown me; it is more than most people will do. But, believe me, there is nothing to be done for the present. The bookies are not likely to be hard upon me, and will be ready to wait for their money. Living abroad on next to nothing, I can gradually pay them off by instalments, and can eventually clear myself. I should be no good at City work; besides, I don't quite like to apply to Jack in a difficulty such as this. As to asking my brother to settle for me on Monday, he would read me a chapter on the folly and vice of gambling, in which he would be well backed up by his wife; and that would be an end of it. There is no use in mincing matters. Much as I hate the idea of leaving the regiment, I must go abroad as soon as ever I can, and try to start a new existence. If ever you think of me at all, you must think of me as the most unlucky fellow you ever came across; that is all. I look upon this as our good-bye for many years to come. I trust your life

will be a happier one than mine—you have everything to make it so. And now let us have a canter
over this nice bit of grass."

Though every member of the party at The Elms
that evening knew more or less what a disastrous
day it had been for one of them, no one could gainsay that George Mansfield was a good loser, and no
trace of those sudden fits of despondency was perceptible in him that on similar occasions are apt to
show themselves in men of softer stuff.

Much has been said and written of late about,
or rather against, the young man of the present day
—his idleness, the effeminacy of his manners, his
recklessness in the pursuit of pleasure or lucre.

Taking, not the individual, but the class as a
whole, we beg leave to question whether these strictures are wholly deserved.

Whenever their country has called upon their
services, these same idle, cigarette-smoking young
fellows, whose literary food consists in not much more
than what their daily sporting papers convey to them;
who are apt to turn up their noses at anything but
the very best '74 champagne, have not been found
wanting.

Was any complaint ever heard when these same
pampered, petted, spoilt children of society were
broiling under an Egyptian sun without any food to
speak of, and with nothing but the slimy water of
the Nile, as thick as pea-soup, to quench their thirst,
and without the prospect of any deed of arms likely
to repay them for their privations?

Can anyone doubt that, should the day ever
arrive when "England expects every man to do his
duty," all these men of pleasure, the habitués of the
race-course and the gambling-table, will be only too
thankful of an excuse for resuming a more active
life, and will be able to prove to any sceptic that in
them there is not much sign of degeneracy as yet?

Should it ever become otherwise—a surmise for
which we see as yet no sort of inclination—the reason
may well be looked for, not so much in idleness or
the search of pleasure, but in the greed for money-
making—to our mind a far more distressing and, at
the same time, more wide-spread symptom amongst
the young generation of the present day.

The West End stockbroker is a modern creation,
and the undoubted success of those who originated
the movement, with remarkable ability and some
means at their disposal, has tempted many others
with scant resources, either intellectual or financial,
to follow in their wake.

Relying upon family interests to procure them
some sort of place in the City, many of them leave
the army, touch up their arithmetic, and are soon
heard holding forth most glibly on an imminent
rise of three-sixteenths in "Tintos" or a slight back-
wardation on "Brighton A's."

Whether they make much money at this business,
if any, is known to nobody but themselves, and is
nobody's concern but their own; but their pale,
hollow cheeks, shattered nerves and ruined constitu-
tions tell an eloquent tale of the wear and tear to

which the incessant pursuit of lucre condemns a frame accustomed to a healthy, open-air life.

Every member of Mrs. Jack Arthur's party seems to agree not to sit up late that evening; and after a certain amount of dawdling about in the garden, and a mild attempt at penny bank, the evening is brought to a close.

George Mansfield, pleading a splitting headache, prefers his own company to that assembled in the smoking-room. He opens the windows wide to let in the balmy night air, laden with the scent of the heliotropes, and, lighting a big cigar, throws himself into the most comfortable armchair he can find.

Yes, the game really is up; at least he is spared the qualms of indecision; he has got to make a clean sweep of everything. He wonders for a moment whether Mildred will have guessed the full extent of the disaster that has befallen him, and whether she understood his expressing doubts as to "staying to the end of the meeting," as intending to convey to her that he might be sailing for the Antipodes within a week's time.

In whichever direction his thoughts turn the outlook is dreary and hopeless. The wrench of leaving his regiment (the — Life Guards) in which he was a general favourite, was a cruel one, and doubly so when it meant at the same time leaving his home, his country—everything, in fact, to which the human heart clings.

What made his reflections doubly galling was the consideration upon how little his fate had depended, and how near he had been reaching what would have been a turning point in his existence. Had Silverstreak just managed to struggle home, his financial difficulties would have been at an end for the time being, and his engagement could have been made public on the following day.

He was not much given to reading poetry, or Lord Lytton's expressive lines might have returned to his memory:

> Yet there's none so unhappy but what he hath been
> Just about to be happy, at some time, I ween;
> And none so beguiled and defrauded by chance,
> But what once in his life some minute circumstance
> Would have fully sufficed to secure him the bliss
> Which, missing it then, he for ever must miss.

How many are there among us in whom these words do not wake some bitter memory?

Why, oh, why did we not, when that little hand lay so trustingly in ours, say the words that were on our lips and that scruples or considerations of some sort held back? No amount of remorse or heartburning will bring back that fugitive moment inscribed in burning letters in our Life's Diary, under the heading of "Opportunities Lost!" Why would we not listen to the advice of a friend who, knowing we had staked far more than was advisable on a forthcoming "certainty," entreated us to hedge on a dark three-year-old of his that was bound to run well, and, as a matter of fact, did win in a canter?

Lucky indeed is he who has no occasion to

supplement these questions by others which may
cause him to meditate on the words:—

> Of all sad words of tongue or pen,
> The saddest are these: "It might have been."

Before he brings his meditations to an end,
George Mansfield decides that anyhow, before many
hours had gone by, Mildred should know the whole
truth—should know that her promise was null and
void; that he to whom it had been made had proved
himself unworthy of her; that before long he might
be little more than a social outcast—one of the
waifs and strays who, under the reign of the survival
of the fittest, had gone to the wall. What would
she say? How would she take this disclosure?

His manhood reasserts itself in the firm resolution not to accept any acts of self-sacrifice from
her. He has ruined his own life, but he will not
ruin hers.

Braced up by this determination, and thereby
reinstated, so to speak, in his own self-respect, he
leaves the consideration of his present financial position and the framing of all further plans until the
morrow, and soon falls asleep from sheer weariness
of mind and body.

He appears at breakfast next morning as cool
and imperturbable as ever, and joins in the discussion of probable winners during the day as if his
mind was free from all care. Soon after he is seen,
with the swinging stride of a Guardsman, betaking
himself to the interview he dreads.

"I hope I am not late; am I? What a jolly morning it is!" are his opening words.

An Englishman's repugnance to anything like melodramatics is so great that no doubt Newgate before now has heard remarks about its being a "nice morning" exchanged within not many yards of the scaffold.

"I am afraid I took the wrong turn after crossing the Windsor Road."

After being set at rest on this score, he plunges *in medias res,* determined not to let his courage ooze out.

She is reclining in a hammock under the shadow of the overhanging boughs of a fir-tree; her expression is sorrowful more than reproachful, and his heart bleeds at the sight of those eyes, dimmed with tears, fixed upon him, not upbraiding or accusing him, but sad and despairing.

He throws himself upon the lawn almost at her feet, presses her hand to his lips and says:

"Darling, you can guess what I have got to tell you; you know that it breaks my heart having to do so; but——"

She interrupts him: "Of course I can guess. Do not accuse yourself, and do not think I am sitting in judgment over you. Don't say another word if it gives you pain; you have suffered quite enough already; it is not for me to add to your trouble. I will only ask you one question, for of course I know but little about betting and money matters generally. Must all be at an end? Is there no hope left? You know what I mean; you know that I would sooner share any hardships with you than withdraw the word I have given you. You know that nothing would seem a sacrifice to me were it done to secure your happiness. Is there no hope?"

He shakes his head. "God knows I have sunk low enough, but not so low as to wish to ruin your life together with mine and to drag you down with me. I have forfeited all right and all claim to your love. Do you remember that morning, years ago, when I first told you that I should marry *you*—or no one? How sweet you looked! I can see you now, in your little cotton frock; do you remember it? How bright and happy all our prospects seemed! I have proved myself unworthy of you."

The terrible earnestness of his tone is even more convincing than his words, and, unwilling to add to his grief by attempting to oppose so firm a resolution, she only says, forcing a smile to her lips, sadder than any outburst of anguish could have been:

"Don't say that, George; you have done nothing unworthy of yourself or of me—nothing that could diminish my respect for you—or anything else."

The effort has been too great, even for her courage, and the words she would have added are buried in an outburst of passionate sobbing.

Utterly unaware of the intrusion they are committing, or otherwise indifferent to it as long as a plentiful supply of small coin, together with some light refreshment in the servants' hall, is forthcoming, a troupe of negro minstrels—that plague of Ascot—

has taken up its position between the house and the
garden, and their discordant voices are soon raised
to the tune of—

"You can do without a wife,
  And you can do without a drink;
  But you cannot do without the merry chink! chink! chink!"

The ludicrousness of this sudden interruption was
too great. Mildred's tears vanished, as if by magic.
She jumped up and exclaimed:

"They are right, George; aren't they? And I am
afraid we have not got the merry 'chink.' Don't let
us say anything more about it: let us be brave and
not think of what might have been. Write and tell
me what your plans are as soon as you get back to
town. By the bye"—and a mischievous smile lighted
up her face—"how is Mrs. Jack Arthur this morning?
It was so stupid of us yesterday, coming and disturb-
ing you, you looked so happy together."

Disappointed by the scant attention bestowed
upon them, and attracted by visions of an unstinted
supply of small beer in the lower regions, the negroes
had slowly disappeared. After one glance in the
direction where a minute ago they stood, George
Mansfield only exclaimed, "Hang Mrs. Jack Arthur!"
and he clasps the girl who has given him so noble
an example of self-sacrificing heroism in his arms,
and their lips meet in one long, passionate embrace.
Then he leaps over the low laurel hedge, and is gone.

CHAPTER III.

"Life! It began with a sigh, grew with the leaves that are
    dead;
 Its pleasures with wings to fly, its sorrows with limbs of lead:
 And rest remaineth never, for the wearier years to be,
 Till the brook shall become a river, and the river become a
    sea."   LORD HOUGHTON.

IN the busy days we live in, people's movements
are no longer regulated by that methodical rigidity
that marked the arrivals and departures of our fore-
fathers. Not much surprise is caused by social
engagements of long standing being overthrown at a
moment's notice, the culprit expressing how "awfully
sorry" he is, at the rate of one half-penny the word.

George Mansfield's announcement on returning,
that he had received a telegram which obliged him
to go to town at once was consequently met with
genuine regret rather than with indignation—many
of the party probably being able to make a shrewd
guess at the real cause of it.

One good point in Mrs. Jack Arthur's nature,
that not even her bitterest enemy could dispute, was
that she was able to hold her tongue; and not a
word had been elicited from her as to anything
George Mansfield told her during their ride on the
previous day.

People were beginning to arrive at the Stands as
he drove past in a rickety fly on his way to Ascot
station. He gave one parting glance on that scene
—to him so familiar and so fond—and wondered,
inwardly, whether his eyes were ever likely to light
on it again. He had no trouble in finding an empty
carriage to take him up to town. In his frame of
mind our fellow-creatures are even more than usually
unwelcome intruders.

His course was now becoming more clear to him.
Before he could make any plans he must break the
matter to his brother, distinctly painful as this process
might be to both parties concerned.

On alighting at the Blenheim Club to order his
luncheon, he did not notice the surprised look of the
waiters at seeing him in town on Cup Day; nor the
deserted look of the club—deserted even by its two
most faithful visitors: the gallant General, the hero
of many a hard fight in the Crimea and in India,
whose genial courtesy of manner is the same, whether
telling his last new anecdote to the Heir-Apparent,
or whether initiating the newly arrived foreign
Attaché, whose looks are as bewildered as his idiom
is unintelligible, into the mysteries of our insular
habits; deserted, also by the handsome, cynical
Colonel, the very type of the *beau sabreur,* with his
heavy moustache—a better judge of a woman's looks
with the one eye he has left, than most men more
favoured in that respect.

Settling himself down at a writing table, George
Mansfield began to realise what an arduous task he

had before him, and nearly an hour had elapsed, and much paper been wasted, before he finally decided upon the following missive:

My DEAR ERRINGTON,—We have not, somehow, seen very much of each other lately, our tastes and ways of living not being the same; and I am afraid I have been rather neglectful about calling on Dorothy.

I am anxious, however, to have a talk with you, if possible, not later than to-morrow, on a serious, and I may at once say a somewhat painful subject. Our conversation will refer to some heavy losses I have recently incurred on the turf, which will in all probability necessitate my leaving the army and this country, for some time at least.

Do not misunderstand me, or suppose I am appealing to your *charity;* but although there has been some estrangement between us of late, it has never, that I know of, taken such proportions that I should decide upon what my future life is to be without your hearing of it.

I have many urgent matters to settle to-morrow; so, unless I hear to the contrary, I will come in for luncheon and we can have a talk afterwards.

Please remember me to Dorothy, and believe me,   Yours affectionately
                                                                          GEORGE.

In case you wish to answer this, the above address will find me.

The town dwelling of the Mansfields was a
gloomy old mansion in St. James's Square, replete
with family portraits of no particular artistic merit,
and cumbersome mahogany furniture, constructed
more with a view to duration than to the comfort of
each successive generation of occupants. Lord Errington and his helpmate were sitting at their dinner-
table, laden with a vast display of Queen Anne plate.
Even the servants officiating around it seemed
thoroughly in keeping with the atmosphere of dull,
old-fashioned respectability that pervaded the whole
dwelling.

Lord Errington was pouring out his glass of after-
dinner claret with some solemnity when the postman's
knock announced the delivery of the last post, and
shortly afterwards his butler, who, like many servants
of the old stamp, carefully petted his master's little
crazes, and looked upon anything that might interfere with the latter's digestion as a most unwarrant-
able disturbance, brought in one solitary letter, and
handed it with a somewhat apologetic look to his
lordship.

"What a bore these letters are, arriving at this
time of night!" exclaims the latter somewhat irritably
across the table to his better half.

Virtue—conjugal, domestic, and maternal but
each of them in its least attractive guise, is plainly
written on Lady Errington's somewhat hard, but not
ill-shaped features. The blameless, but pleasureless
life she had led, and on which she prided herself—
the oft-recurring cares of maternity, the daily inter-

course with a selfish, narrow-minded man, given to finding fault with everyone indiscriminately, had gradually, between them, produced the effect of her taking a somewhat stern and gloomy view of the world in general. Knowing little or nothing of the pleasures of life, she felt but scant sympathy for those more given to look upon the brighter side of human existence.

Consequently, her brother-in-law, George, had never been a favourite with her. His cheery way of taking life, with all its ups and downs, grated upon her nerves. His knack of putting in a kind word when Lady Errington was dealing out stern and implacable justice to all offenders—especially those against the Seventh Commandment, a class for whom she knew no mercy or pity—savoured to her of laxity of morals, of defending sin, or, as she was apt to put it, "doing the work of Satan." How she reconciled the severity of her strictures upon those of her sisters whose life of storm and stress had been to hers what the Niagara is to a Dutch canal with the texts she was anxious to quote on all occasions, must be left to her to decide.

Lord Errington takes the letter from the salver; notices that it is marked "Immediate;" sends for his spectacles, and, the servants having retired, he reads his brother's missive aloud, slowly and deliberately, but without interrupting it with a word of comment.

The first remark he makes on getting to the end is characteristic of the man: "Isn't the Bishop of Nottingham lunching here to-morrow, dear?"

"Of course he is; so *that* will never do. What is to become of this poor abandoned man?" she goes on in a fretful tone. "He must have taken leave of his senses. You will see that, in spite of all he says about not requiring charity, he will try and get round you. As if we had no children to provide for!" And she takes a sort of mental survey of her numerous offspring.

This exemplary couple agreed on most things; never did they do so more fully than that George must be told that his brother would be very happy to assist him with his influence and an unlimited amount of advice, but that his duties towards his children precluded him "from taking the eventuality into consideration of reducing the latter's patrimony in order to settle their uncle's betting accounts."

The letter was followed by a postscript:—

"Dorothy wishes me to add that, as the Bishop of Nottingham is lunching with us to-morrow, you will no doubt prefer coming in rather later. You will find me in the morning-room from three p.m."

With his hopes not unduly raised as to the results of the forthcoming interview, George Mansfield kept the appointment thus ungraciously granted. He was by no means surprised at the querulous tone of his brother's remarks, which may be summed up in frequent references to his numerous offspring and the now consummated realisation of his former predictions.

"All I can do," he wound up by saying, "is to try to get you some sort of appointment; and if you manage to put by a little year by year, I dare say your creditors will not care to get you into the Bankruptcy Court. Of course, there are not very many appointments for which you would be qualified. I believe they pay a Queen's messenger three hundred a-year to travel all over Europe with a carpet-bag full of despatches which interest nobody but the man who wrote them; I might see if I could get something of that sort for you."

The half-contemptuous tone with which these words were uttered was rather too much for the other's patience and forbearance.

"You are really quite too kind," he answered, "and I am so much obliged for your high opinion of my capacities in thinking me capable of conveying a carpet-bag to Constantinople and back; but I don't think I shall have to trouble you. I hope to be able to obtain a commission in some foreign army, and, should that fail, I shall have to try gold-digging in South Africa."

With this, the interview was brought to a close, Lord Errington's firm behaviour earning him the most unlimited approval of his better half, who congratulated him most warmly on the conscientious manner in which he had fulfilled this painful duty.

The next few days were amongst the most trying ones in poor George Mansfield's chequered existence. It was gall and wormwood to his straightforward nature to have to admit to his creditors his absolute inability to meet his engagements for the present; and though most of them were willing to take his word as to future settlement and to abstain from taking any steps against him—there is more kindheartedness amongst that much-abused class of bookmakers than many indignant paterfamiliases imagine—nevertheless, he went through many a painful moment infinitely wounding to his pride.

Some weeks have elapsed. Highly recommended by his superior officers, George Mansfield at last saw some prospect of obtaining a commission in the Austrian Cavalry, considerable influence having been brought to bear in the matter from high quarters.

Much correspondence had to be gone through and numerous questions answered, the extreme punctiliousness of the military code of honour in Continental armies making it indispensable for him to prove that he was leaving his regiment entirely of his own free will, without any sort of slur upon his character as an officer and a gentleman, and only when this had been investigated and sifted to the entire satisfaction of all the foreign military author-ities, was the difficulty of nationality got over, and George Mansfield duly gazetted as "sub-lieutenant to the 24th Regiment of Austrian Lancers," with the prospect of becoming lieutenant after an interval of some months, which would enable him to acquaint himself with the language of his regiment.

CHAPTER IV.

"Yes, thou art gone! and round me, too, the night,
  In ever-nearing circles, weaves her shade.
I see her veil draw soft across the day:
  I feel her slowly-chilling breath invade
The cheek grown thin, the brown hair sprent with grey;
  I feel her finger light
Laid pausefully upon life's headlong train;
  The foot less prompt to meet the morning dew,
The heart less bounding at emotion new,
  And hope once crush'd, less quick to spring again."
                              MATTHEW ARNOLD.

THE severe trials our hero had been going
through during the last weeks and months produced
a beneficial effect upon his character. Many men
of softer stuff might well have broken down, and
would have relapsed into a state of complete mental
prostration, or given up a hopeless struggle. George
Mansfield might possibly have been tempted to do
so during some of the bitterest moments of these
intervening weeks, had it not been that whenever his
spirit seemed to fail him, he would be sure to find
words of comfort and encouragement in the one
quarter in which he sought them—from Mildred
Charteris.

True to her love, hopeless though it might be,
the latter had with admirable tact and sagacity

played to him the part of confidant and adviser,
listening with unflagging interest to the account of
all his alternate hopes and disappointments; advising
him as much as lay in her power, always bright,
hopeful and sympathising. Her affection for him
was so utterly unselfish that she never stopped to
think what her life would be after his departure,
and how short-lived this present happiness must be.

The season had run its course; people were
leaving town, or those who were unable to do so
pretended to be on the point of leaving, or had their
departure chronicled in the *Morning Post.* In the
first week of August Mildred had accompanied her
aunt, who devoted most of her time to the motherless girl, to a little riverside house, not far from
Marlow, where the latter was in the habit of spending
two or three summer months.

About that time George Mansfield came to the
conclusion that all his preparations had been made,
and that he could only delay his departure by shallow pretences. He was beginning to resign himself
almost cheerfully to his fate, as far as he was personally concerned; and the dark hours through which
he passed were caused by no selfish considerations.
The thought of what Mildred's future would be,
once he had left, weighed heavily upon his mind,
and caused him many an hour of bitter self-reproach.
He fully realised how utterly hopeless his own prospects were, and he decided, in an almost Quixotic
spirit of self-abnegation, to use all his influence upon
her, in order that she should wipe out the past, no

matter what suffering it might entail upon him, if only he could thereby ensure her happiness.

The days of chivalry are over, we are told in letters freely admitted during the silly season to the columns of the daily press. Far be it from us to contradict what appears to be the general consensus of middle-class public opinion; but are not the exceptions sufficiently numerous to form, at least, a very respectable minority? And is it not doubly meritorious if, in this age of snobbishness, of greedy money-making, of sickening little flirtations, the offspring of vanity and idleness, any vestige of chivalrous feeling should have survived in the men of the present young generation? What is their experience of women—or ladies, we should say? We take it the following is a pretty fair and not overdrawn sample of the first stage of a young man's love-making—save the mark—in a London ball-room:—

He: "Lady ——, do come down and have some supper before the rush begins—won't you?"

She: "All right, I don't mind; although I am not sure I did not promise Harry [her 'young man'] to go down with him. Anyhow, we won't stay away long."

He (taking her arm): "That is an awfully nice frock you have got on to-night."

She: "I am so glad you like it, for I am sure you know all about it. [Being firmly convinced that he knows as much about female attire as she does about astronomy.] •You have no idea what a row Dick [her husband] made when the bill came in!"

He: "Did he really? How brutal of him! Now, I am sure if I were married I should always like my wife to be the best-dressed woman in the room—at least, I would if *you* were my wife."

She: "What nonsense! As if you would ever look at me!"

He: "Look at you! I should think I would!" [Accompanied by an expressive glance.]

She: "So you imagine. You would soon get tired of me; all men are alike. I suppose you are no better than the rest. By the way, if you are not going to Sandown to-morrow, do come in and see me about tea-time; I am sure to be alone, as everybody will be out of town."

He, maliciously: "How about Harry?"

She: "What nonsense you do talk. I have known Harry all my life; he is a sort of brother to me. (Ahem!) But don't come if you don't like."

He: "All right. I'll come right enough about six, or that sort of thing."

And now we repeat the question: is it not most meritorious if any spark of respect or chivalry or nobler feeling towards the other sex remain in the heart beating under the white gardenia of the "masher" after hearing what he hears and seeing what he sees every day of his life?

And for all that, do we not all of us know men who have sacrificed, all but too willingly, every prospect they had in the world—fortune, fame and family—for the sake of a woman? Are there not many more who stint themselves, who give up a season's hunting or yachting, or any favourite pastime they have, to make up the deficit in Delilah's budget? The cynic may shrug his shoulders; and well he may, for men who do this sort of thing are not much given to talking about it.

A lovely morning towards the end of August. Sheltered from the rays of the sun by the branches of an overhanging beech, a punt is made fast against the bank in one of the back-waters close to Hurley Lock.

The expression of the occupants of it is sadly in contrast with the brightness of the scenery around them. The man is the first to break the silence.

"I suppose this is our last day together for a long time to come. This is my final good-bye to you and to the river, and all the rest of it. Mildred, I have been wishing to have a long talk with you for some time back. Perhaps I ought to have spoken sooner, but somehow I could not. I wish to thank you for all you have done for me during these last weeks and months. You have been my guardian angel; without you I was hopelessly lost and stranded. I do not wish to show my gratitude in words, but in deeds. That moment has now come. Darling! since that awful day at Ascot you have known the whole truth, haven't you? Perhaps I should have told you of it again, but anyhow you know that it would be the wildest and most criminal folly on my part ever to hope of making you my wife. I played for high stakes and lost. I have thought it over in my mind many and many a time, and it cannot be. Don't ask me any questions; don't try to shake my resolution! I should not love you as I do, were I to ask you to become the wife of a penniless outcast. But this is not all. It is not at a moment such as this that I shall play a part and pretend not to know that you do care for me very, very much." (She nods assent.) "Well, in spite of all that, this is what I want to tell you. Now comes the painful moment. Of course you are nothing but a child; you have your whole life before you. I do not wish to spoil it. We should have been happy together, should not we? I feel sure you will never care for anybody else in quite the same way—the thought would kill me—but you must not spend your life as a homeless, lonely orphan on my account. I have thought it over well—never mind what my feelings are; I have forfeited the right to have any—but for your sake, listen to my parting words. If old Devereux asks you to become his wife, which he may do any day, do not refuse him on my account. There, I have said what I meant to say, and it has been rather more painful even than I had anticipated; but I have done my duty, as I hope always to do in future."

For some seconds, that seemed to him like so many hours, no answer is forthcoming; not a sound is heard but that of the water rushing down the neighbouring weir mingled with that of the breeze passing through the leaves already coloured with the glowing tints of autumn.

The tears are in Mildred's eyes, but there is no tremor in her voice when she answers:

"Of course, darling, I know everything. God knows I would willingly face every privation for your sake, and think myself thrice happy to do so. But it must not be; I should only be hampering you. Without me you still have many chances in your favour; with me you would have none. I know you mean it kindly, all you say to me about Lord Devereux; I know what it must have cost you saying it; don't think me ungrateful, therefore, if I wish these words had been left unsaid. I have made up my mind to part with you, but not to sell myself to the highest bidder. Don't think me cruel, for of course you meant it kindly. Do you remember the little ring you gave me once, long, long ago? You shall have it back to wear on your watch-chain; and whenever you care for any other woman, throw it into the nearest river you can find. Good-bye!"

He takes the ring, and one last embrace seals their compact.

Not many hours later, after a hearty farewell from Mildred's Aunt, George Mansfield was whirling back into town.

CHAPTER V.

"One fond kiss and then we sever,
One farewell and then for ever,
Deep, in heart-wrung tears I'll pledge thee,
Warring sighs and groans I'll wage thee."

R. BURNS.

EVEN between such an exemplary, well-assorted couple as are Lord and Lady Errington it must not be supposed that the friction of everyday life does not occasionally engender a few sparks, speedily extinguished though they may be.

Supposing there is no occasion for any misgivings as to the equilibrium of the budget, what are the chief objections of a man against embarking on matrimony?

1. Giving up his independence. In this respect the chances are that if he marries a girl who has been in hard training for three or four seasons in London, she will not be over-exacting and will act upon the principle of "do ut des."

2. Having to go out every evening. Sooner than he anticipates he will be accommodated by his wife suggesting going out without him.

3. Last and least amongst his objections will be: that his wife might get into a fast set and take to flirting.

His chief troubles, if any, are, according to our belief, more likely to arise from a totally different quarter.

Supposing, for example, after a few months of matrimonial bliss, he drops in at his club before dinner for a quiet game of bézique and loses enough, not to affect his income, but only his temper. He returns to his Penates and, after dressing in a hurry —a severe trial to most men's nerves—is met with hardly quite as smiling a countenance as he fondly hoped to see.

"How late you are, dear!" are the words he is received with (this epithet of "dear" amongst husbands and wives is generally used on the *lucus a non lucendo* principle). "If it bores you dining at home, I wish you would say so, for Jennie (her sister) asked me to dine and do a play with her. I suppose we had better go down; dinner has been announced for the last ten minutes."

Soup—rather cold—is eaten in silence, then during a temporary disappearance of the servants, when the culprit is thinking he is going to have a quiet little chat with his *uxor amans* on all sorts of pleasant topics, the latter addresses him with a tone of great urbanity but no less great decision:

"You must really speak seriously to Johnson (the butler); he is out all day. When I came home this afternoon there was only one footman to let me in. It really is too bad."

Duly impressed with the gravity of such an occurrence, the husband meekly replies:

"All right, dear. I will certainly speak to him; in fact, if you like, I will send him away." (The individual referred to having been with him for the last ten years and hitherto having been considered an invaluable servant.)

Conversation somewhat flags, for it is a curious phenomenon how easily an atmospheric disturbance is created on the matrimonial horizon and how much patience and perseverance is required to quell it and to restore the glass to "set fair."

She soon opens fire again:

"Of course I don't suppose you have any idea whether you ever paid last quarter's rates and taxes yet; they came bothering me about them again to-day. That sort of thing is such a nuisance when one is writing one's letters. Perhaps you had better let me do it in future."

He replies blandly:

"By all means, you shall if you like. As a matter of fact, I don't believe I have paid them."

And so on *ad nauseam.*

Thus it came to pass that on one particular evening towards the end of August, the perfect harmony that generally prevailed at the Priory—the ancestral home of the Mansfield family—suffered a temporary disturbance.

Lord Errington was within the very narrow limits that his essentially unloving nature allowed, not altogether devoid of affection for his brother, and the fact that the latter had made no appeal whatever to his liberality had produced a somewhat softening effect upon his heart.

In his weaker moments he could not but reproach himself for the scant measure of support he had offered his brother in so severe a crisis, and like a true man, he took his wife to task on the subject.

Petty natures like his are apt to look for support to back up their own opinions, and then, when their object is achieved, to fall foul of those whose assistance not long ago they craved for.

A good opening is afforded him by some very severe strictures passed by his wife upon some slight breach of the rules of household economy that has come to her knowledge, and he opens fire at once:

"My dear Dorothy, it is all very well not to encourage waste, and I highly appreciate your good qualities in that as in every respect. On the other hand, even good qualities may be carried to an excess, and even supposing they did, as you say, eat last night's dessert in the housekeeper's room, we shall not be in the workhouse for that. In fact, I wish to take this opportunity for calling your attention to the danger you are in of pushing economy too far. It was chiefly owing to your influence that I declined helping poor George in any way, and it has frequently occurred to me since that I should have done better to have acted more upon my own judgment in the matter."

A rather angry retort follows this aggressive

movement, and most of the evening is spent with what may be described by the homely term of a family jar, through which there is no occasion for us to follow this estimable couple. Anyhow, before prayers are said and the lights put out, Lord Errington remains in possession of the battle-field, and an agreement has been come to that a cheque for five hundred pounds is to be sent next morning to his brother in order to give him a fair start abroad.

The latter is completely taken back at receiving this donation, accompanied by some words of farewell that are warmer than anything he anticipated, and it is, though with a heavy heart, nevertheless in a state of peace and good-will with all men that he lay down for the very last time in his snug little chambers in St. James' Street.

*　　*　　*　　*　　*　　*　　*

Scene: Victoria Station, London, Chatham and Dover Railway, 2.50 p.m.

The present generation is proverbially disinclined to waste time at railway stations, this disinclination being in most cases in inverse ratio to the value of the time of the persons thus affected to themselves, or anyhow to the world in general.

It is thus about ten minutes only before the departure of the Club train that George Mansfield is seen dashing up. Before he has time almost to answer the stereotyped question of "Where for, sir?" his eye catches sight of a well-known face and figure; for, pale as death, and utterly unconscious of the bustle and excitement around her, Mildred Charteris is standing on the platform to bid God-speed to him.

Fortunately, leave-takings at railway stations do not form part of our social code of etiquette, though they are much in vogue abroad. Huge gatherings of friends, armed with floral offerings, presumably corresponding in dimensions to the feelings of the donors, are no unusual occurrence at Continental railway stations. The inconvenience of these demonstrations is sufficiently illustrated by the recent fate of a very fascinating visitor to one of the German watering-places, whose bright eyes had done considerable havoc in the neighbourhood, and had presumably interfered in many cases with the salutary, soothing effect of the Ferdinands-Quelle. Be this as it may, she was obliged to see her train steam out of the station, being unable to extricate herself from the bouquets her admirers had been showering with too lavish a hand into her carriage when she drove up in the last moment.

What can be more painful than that mixture of the sublime and the trivial! The leave-taking may be from what is dearest upon earth, amidst jostling porters, struggling materfamiliases in search of the next train for Margate, 'Arrys nudging each other and whispering, "Oh my, don't she look cut up!" the whole relieved by an occasional whistle, or the letting-off of steam.

You are, as likely as not, vowing eternal fidelity, when your servant comes up: "Beg your pardon, sir; will you have the dressing-bag with you in the

4*

carriage?" You are settling where her next letter
can reach you, only to be interrupted by an official
blandly inquiring whether he "might trouble you for
your ticket," and so forth.

We will, therefore, leave our poor hero and
heroine to their somewhat disjointed adieux. Their
feelings might well be described in Heine's sad and
pathetic words:

> Wir haben nicht geweinet,
> Wir seufzten nicht Weh und nicht Ach,
> Die Seufzer und die Thränen
> Die kamen hintennach.

FEW things are more depressing than a long
railway journey in solitude. The first hour or two
there may be a sort of feeling of relaxation—a sensation that, for better, for worse, the die is cast; that
the decision taken before starting can now no longer
be reversed; that no scope is left for any activity
whatever, and that the hard-worked brain and body
may take a well-earned rest. The chances are,
however, that this sensation will be a short-lived one;
for the impossibility of any physical exercise will
mostly set the mind to work all the harder; and we
fancy many rash resolutions have been engendered
during a sleepless night in a railway carriage.

Utter depression and prostration had seized upon
poor George Mansfield's mind as he was whirled
along through the slums of Battersea and the gloomy
darkness of the tunnel that passes under the Crystal
Palace, and it came as a welcome relief to him when

at last his meditations were interrupted by the shrill cry of, "This way for the boat, please!"

It is of course a commonplace truism disputed by no one, that women have far greater power of resistance against physical pain than the sterner sex can boast of. Have we not all of us seen many a time, pale, delicate women, with highly-strung nerves, tortured by a racking headache, sitting through the dullest of dinner-parties at the fag-end of a London season, in a temperature of about ninety degrees, with an elderly neighbour pouring forth vague platitudes into their unwilling ears, the poor victims, with temples throbbing, responding with the blandest smile, wishing, oh, so earnestly! the said elderly gentleman at the bottom of the sea and themselves in bed with an unlimited supply of sal-volatile.

Whether this applies to the same extent to mental suffering may possibly be disputed by some. Anyhow, the next weeks and months that followed, gave Mildred Charteris ample opportunity of showing that indomitable pluck and stubbornness of spirit which is frequently found in a well-bred woman.

Brought up as an orphan, without all the petting and spoiling an only child generally comes in for, her character had been given an early opportunity of developing itself; and the habit of thinking and judging for herself had grown upon her at a time of life when many other girls would be incapable of even ordering a frock without assistance.

Outwardly, nothing was altered in her existence. Her manner was as genial and cheery as ever. But as days and weeks followed each other, she could not at times ward off a feeling of intense loneliness. George's letters came irregularly, by fits and starts. The beginning of an entirely new existence, with its manifold phases of an activity altogether novel to him, every detail of which he entered into with all his heart and soul, left him but little time for retrospection. Minute accounts of all the passing impressions that struck his mind were more prevalent than queries as to her life; and although she made every allowance for this under the circumstances, she could not at times resist a slight feeling of disappointment.

Why is it that so many women belonging to what is termed a "fast set" should, besides their many friends and kindred spirits, almost invariably endeavour to have in their orbit some young girl, irreproachable in manner and tone, whose presence at a dinner-table quells the very possibility of anything in the shape of a double-entendre, and gives a transient look of intense respectability to the whole proceedings? It is believed that on such occasions, previous notice is given to the habitués that they will have to behave themselves, as "Miss So-and-So is dining"—with the option of not coming if they do not feel up to the task. Anyhow, it is a thing by no means uncommon to see this intimacy between an exceedingly flighty matron and a maiden the very emblem of propriety.

Should the latter be questioned or any doubts be expressed as to the expediency of this great

intimacy, she will probably reply: "Oh, yes; I know
people say a lot of ill-natured things about poor
Florence; but I am sure there is no harm in her.
She is so good-natured, and she has always been so
nice to me!" The latter remark will probably be true
in the sense that the said Florence is too much a
woman of the world not to be very careful as to
what she says to and before her friend; so that the
chances of any contamination for the latter are not
nearly so great as might appear at first sight.

Thus it happened one evening, early in the
season, that, arriving at a ball almost at the same
time as Miss Charteris, Mrs. Jack Arthur had addressed her in the cloak-room, without waiting for
any more formal introduction, and an acquaintance
was then and there formed. Mrs. Jack soon took a
strong fancy to the motherless girl; she admired her
frank and fearless manner, the independence of her
mind, and her utter contempt for anything in the
shape of social prejudices. Are we not all of us
given to appreciate more especially those qualities in
others in which we feel ourselves deficient? Her
first advances rather took Mildred by surprise, and
she consulted George Mansfield as to the measure in
which he wished her to respond to them. The latter
was then in the very heyday of his short but very
enjoyable career: and, like most thoroughly idle men,
he was in a perpetual hurry; moreover, the question
did not, in his mind, suggest much matter for de-
liberation.

"Go to the Opera with Mrs. Jack?" was his

reply: "I certainly would if I were you—the De
Reszkes are singing, and everybody will be there. I
dare say people have told you a lot of nonsense
about her, but she is an awfully kind-hearted little
woman. By all means, go. Of course, I don't mean
that I want you to make a bosom friend of her. I
am afraid I *must* be off now!"

Having thus obtained the only sanction she stood
in need of, Mildred hesitated no longer. Her genuine
love of music made a night at the Opera a real treat
to her, and not infrequently during the season was
she seen in Mrs. Jack's pit-tier box. Thus a sort of
outward friendship sprang up, without, of course, any
real intimacy, for which the most elementary conditions were wanting.

One of the prominent features in Mrs. Jack's
little entertainments was Captain—alias "Jim"—
Atherstone, who occupied the proud position of being
what the world would call Mrs. Jack's "young man."
(Is it not a pity that this denomination should ever
have been appropriated from the servants' hall?)
Poor Jim! It may be questioned whether his fate
was always an enviable one. To be ordered about,
and told to get up a river or other party, at no
matter how short notice, whenever it might suit Mrs.
Jack's gracious pleasure; to be made to throw over
all engagements whenever a note might arrive saying
she wanted another man for dinner: to be in a state
of servile dependency, and yet to be expected to
rattle the chains of captivity for proud delight at
being allowed to wear them; such was his fate!

What made his case an exceptionally severe one was
that, practically, his servitude lasted all the year
round, being a country neighbour of the Arthurs.
Good-looking and cheery, he was voted by everybody
a real good fellow, a view, no doubt, not unfavour-
ably affected by the fact that he had some twenty
thousand pounds a-year of his own.

Since the end of the season Mildred had been
without news from Mrs. Jack (she had not yet got
herself to call her by her Christian name), but her
surprise was not an altogether disagreeable one on
receiving, early in October, a note unmistakably addressed in the latter's bold, legible hand. It ran
thus—

MY DEAR MILDRED,--I am afraid you must be
having a dull time of it, for I hear you have refused
all invitations to Scotland on account of your aunt's
health. I wonder if I shall be more lucky. I want
you *so badly* to come down on the 30th for a few
days. No party, or I should not dare ask you without a chaperone: only Mrs. Ryder and her two
daughters, little Lady Sinclair (who was married the
other day), the Wharnhills and a few men. I won't
tell you who the men are till you are here. One of
them is awfully anxious to see you. Do come!
Oakley is our station, the 2.35 from St. Pancras our
best train.

Yours ever,
KATE ARTHUR.

Mildred's first impulse was to write a polite but firm refusal, saying she could not very well make an exception, having declined all other engagements: or something to that purpose. A sudden change for the better in her aunt's health, together with the arrival of a distant connection, who, for the time being, was able to take her place, however, were two arguments in favour of allowing herself to be persuaded that a little change would do her good; and thus she found herself, on the day appointed, driving up to the door of Manor Lodge, the Leicestershire fastness of the Arthur family.

CHAPTER VI.

"And be my most gain'd, your least given if such
Your sweet will be! I reckon not the cost,
Nor count the gain by little or by much,
Or least or most."

ARRIVING by oneself in a country-house, even with
a solemn promise of finding no party, is rather shy
work for a girl not yet out of her teens, particularly
when a Babel of tongues emerging from the hall
where tea was being poured out to the men just
returned from shooting, has a tendency to shake her
confidence in the value of that promise.

Mrs. Jack greeted her with effusive cordiality,
hoped she wasn't tired, inquired after her aunt and
went through the necessary introductions in the most
approved style.

Mildred was pretty quick at taking in impressions, and a rapid survey told her that in addition
to those mentioned in the letter of invitation she
had received, Mrs. Jack had only asked one or two
country neighbours; so she couldn't help wondering
how comparatively such a small number of people
contrived to make so much noise as she was coming in.

The faces of Mrs. Ryder and her two daughters
were familiar to her, and she mentally put them

down as a most uninteresting family. The mother
a comely widow with some remains of beauty, that
at its prime must have been surpassing; the eldest
girl, tall and showy, with good features, lovely hair
and a slim waist, well turned out and decidedly re-
presentative; the girl was never known to say the
wrong thing or seen talking to the wrong person.
In fact, Miss Ryder, before expressing an opinion on
any given subject, may be excepting the weather,
generally made sure of ascertaining in which direction the consensus of opinion lay, or else shrouded
herself in safe conventionalisms.

Mrs. Ryder's youngest daughter had, before she
left the nursery, learnt the lesson that her part in
life was to act as a foil to her more brilliant sister,
and that her share of the good things would be that
which her sister chose to leave her. Poor girl! she
accepted this position with commendable resignation
and unfaltering good humour.

The tall, fair woman, playing bézique at the other
end of the room with Jim Atherstone, Mildred quickly
recognises as Lady Wharnhill, Mrs. Jack's particular
friend and confidante, who, when the Arthurs, after
their great coup in copper, emigrated from Bayswater
to the Marble Arch, had held out a helping hand
to Mrs. Jack, a service the latter was not likely to
forget.

Gossip-mongers will have it that when her lord
and master has an exceptionally bad week's racing,
Mrs. Jack's gratitude towards her takes a somewhat
tangible shape in order to keep the pot boiling in

the Wharnhill establishment, but we will have nothing to do with their reckless assertions, all the less so as there is not a more popular man in London than Charlie Wharnhill.

Somehow you cannot help liking him. There is a sort of irresistible charm in his manner, which disarms anyone who might be disposed to say unkind things about him.

He is standing with his back to the fire; there is a good-humoured twinkle in his brown eyes as he listens, apparently with profound interest, to the dissertations of his neighbour, a foreign minister with almond-shaped eyes, the darkest complexion and the whitest teeth ever seen on this island of ours, on the probable winner of the Cesarewitch.

Charlie Wharnhill had forgotten more about racing than the other ever knew, and could, with very few words, have demolished the structure of the newly-created Excellency's arguments, but he is constitutionally too good-natured, or else too indolent, to enter upon a discussion, still less to contradict anybody. So he only gives the distinguished foreigner a vigorous slap on his broad, round shoulders (an act of familiarity which the easy-going manner and the unprecedented popularity of the latter fully justify) and says:

"All right, old man. You go and plank it down on the mare—as long as I need not," he adds after half a second's pause.

He then moves to the farther side of the room and gives the ladies a turn. They are mostly dis-

posed to give him a hearing, and his soft, gentle
manner, together with a singularly pleasant voice,
seem at once to bring him nearer to the object he
is bestowing his attention upon. Somehow you can't
help at once "feeling at home with Charlie" is what
they say of him.

"Who is the lady in the sealskin jacket just come
in?" says Mildred to Mrs. Jack.

"Oh! my dear, don't you know Mrs. Garrard?
She lives close by. She is such a dear; she was a
Miss Powell—Irish, of course. I am sure you will
like her, so try and make friends with her."

Whatever Mildred's wishes and intentions may be
in this respect, no opportunity is offered her for carrying them out, as the dressing gong is sounding, putting an end to the rather languishing conversation
by the tea-table and the forty winks which most of
the men are indulging in in the smoking-room.

Having gained her room Mildred involuntarily
asked herself the question: "I wonder really what I
came here for? I should not be surprised if it was
going to be very dull; anyhow, I won't stay longer
than Friday."

These reflections, we take it, are rather frequently
made on very insufficient evidence on arriving at a
country-house, and in many cases those who made
them would be much surprised a week afterwards
to be reminded of them. At any rate, Mildred makes
up her mind that no one of her own sex amongst
the party is likely to be much of a resource to her,

though, of course, she has not yet seen most of the men.

Like a model host Mr. Arthur arrives downstairs before his guests. There is nothing striking about the man, as he stands in front of the fire looking complacently around at all the pretty things his wife's undeniable taste has collected in her drawing-room— nothing whatever to catch the eye. Even his age would be hard to guess; it might be anything between thirty-five and fifty. The lines on his brow are suggestive of much hard work during his early life; but, though honest John Arthur had, so to speak, risen from the ranks, there was little if anything in his manner to betray him. Whatever his birth might have been, he was a gentleman by nature, or shall we say by intuition; and no truer word was ever said, than when one of his wife's friends exclaimed one day: "Isn't he extraordinary, that fellow Arthur; he ought to be a snob, if anybody is, but somehow he isn't!"

His affection and admiration for his wife are extreme—so great as to materially dim the brightness of his judgment in everything she is concerned in. Her friends are for the most part only *his* in the sense that they drink his champagne, smoke his cigars, ride his horses and make love to his wife.

People are gradually straggling in: the men anxious to get near the fire and not be kept waiting moreover determined to reserve their conversational powers until dinner is announced.

As Mildred stepped into the drawing-room she

was fairly taken aback at being met at the doorway
by no other than Lord Devereux, evidently on the
look-out for her, smiling and radiant and on the
best of terms with himself and the world in general.
Her feelings on being greeted with outstretched hand
by her veteran admirer were somewhat divided. In
one way it was a comfort meeting at least one old
friend amongst a party of comparative strangers; on
the other hand, the thought at once flashed across
her mind: "Of course he will begin the same old
story over again at once." Nevertheless she responded with a fair amount of alacrity to his greeting, and being taken in to dinner by Jim Atherstone,
was not affected pleasantly or otherwise at seeing
Lord Devereux settling himself down as her left-hand
neighbour.

Boys and elderly men, once they are far gone on
any particular object of their affection, are proverbially apt to make great fools of themselves; but there
are no doubt exceptions, and Lord Devereux flattered
himself that he had himself pretty well "in hand."
Anyhow, nothing in his demeanour would have struck
a casual observer that his battered old heart was, all
through dinner, beating at an accelerated rate against
his well starched white waistcoat when his eyes rested
upon Mildred, who was looking her very best in a
white Empire dress of a soft, clinging material, con-
fined at the waist by a broad pink sash, and with
large velvet sleeves of the same delicate hue.

After weeks of seclusion society in itself is a sort
of restorative, quite apart from the intrinsic conver-

sational powers of those by whom it is represented;
and before long Mildred found herself rattling away
merrily on very ordinary topics with Jim Atherstone,
who she soon found had got more to say for himself
than she had ever given him credit for. Lord Devereux
waited patiently, and when an opportunity was offered
him, the remarks he made were well within the
range of what any old friend might have felt justified
in saying.

On returning to the drawing-room Miss Charteris,
mindful of her hostess's injunctions, made a point of
getting introduced to Mrs. Garrard, and soon settled
down in a sofa by her side. She had not been talking five minutes before she said to herself: "What a
nice little woman!" Before the men had returned
she had gone further and had decided to make a
friend of her. A small head, carried rather erect on
well shaped, sloping shoulders; a slim and graceful
figure; tiny hands that would not be credited with
being able to "hold" many a hard-pulling hunter
that has sent home good men and true with aching
backs and limbs; hair of a rich warm tint, such as
no lotion that ever left the great Lentheric's laboratory
can produce—these are the points that strike the
eye resting for the first time on Mrs. Garrard's slender
and intensely refined form. No fear of any deceit
or treachery lurking behind those eyes, that are
neither grey nor blue, and that look at you so frankly
and fearlessly from under the dark and delicately
pencilled brows. Cares and troubles have given them
a somewhat serious and pensive look, but this is often

cast aside when their owner's true Hibernian sense of humour bursts forth in merriment. How brightly those pensive eyes will shine and sparkle when hounds are running across the Belvoir Vale, and she, on Torpedo, is well to the front! How maliciously they will twinkle when one of her would-be admirers is professing his willingness to lay his heart at her little feet! No breath of scandal has ever touched her, and with rare tact she has always contrived to keep as friends even those who had at one time professed warmer feelings for her.

Married when little more than a child to a light-hearted and somewhat scatter-brained captain of dragoons, she had discovered before she was out of her teens that life for her was not likely to be free from rocks and quicksands. Her marriage had not turned out a happy one, for Captain Garrard's genuine and even passionate devotion to his wife had not been enough to keep him out of mischief. Restless and impulsive by nature, he had, after two or three years of married life, started off for Canada with some vague notion of making a fortune cattle-ranching, and but little had been heard of him since. Thus he left his wife alone in the world with a considerably reduced income and a somewhat difficult part to play.

Her one distraction during the many troubles of her short married life had been her genuine love of hunting, and to this pursuit she determined to remain faithful. A distant connection, with nothing particular to do in the world, agreed to settle down with her,

and Addesleigh Vicarage soon became the unpretend-
ing but thoroughly comfortable and attractive little
home of Mrs. Garrard and her maiden aunt. People
began to know her ways, and before long she was a
universal favourite, even in a country not much given
to taking up strangers. After two or three of the
most enterprising amongst the men had been put in
their places somewhat roundly ("She won't stand any
nonsense, I can tell you!" was the account of one of
her crestfallen admirers), she had nothing more to
complain of; and seeing her remarkable judgment
and boldness with hounds, her friends took to offer-
ing her mounts whenever she cared to have them—
a far more acceptable offer than that commodity of
rather questionable value called their love. Putting
aside even the almost faultless mould of her features,
her great attraction lay in the extreme refinement
and softness of her expression, and the sweetness of
her smile. "Why, to see that woman smile," an enthusiastic countryman of hers once said, "is enough
to charm the very birds from off the trees!"

Though not much given to jumping at conclusions, Mildred felt herself powerfully attracted, and
before the evening was over she had ceased regretting
having accepted Mrs. Jack's invitation.

The next few days passed on pleasantly enough
for Miss Charteris. Two women — *nice* women, at
least— once they begin a real friendship, do not keep
many secrets from each other long, presumably from
the fact that they have no secrets to blush over.
Safe under her friend's wing, it was easier for Mildred

to ward off Lord Devereux's attentions, and she was
beginning really to hope that her visit would pass off
without his lordship's going on his knees before
her, literally or metaphorically.

In this, however, she was doomed to disappointment. Days were going by, and Mildred had given
in to Mrs. Jack's entreaties to prolong her visit into
the beginning of the following week. By this time
Lord Devereux was beginning to get rather restless
and anxious to get it over and to know his fate; so
one evening, he made a point after dinner of occupying an empty seat next to the object of his affection,
who had imprudently seated herself rather apart from
the rest of the company.

"Miss Charteris," he began, "I find I am obliged
to go up to town to-morrow morning; so this is my
last and only chance of asking you a question which
has been on my lips for months back. I am past
the age of melodramatics, and I feel sure that I
should only injure whatever little chance I may have
by making any pretty speeches at so grave a moment. Will you be my wife? Before you answer let
me add only very few words. You have known this
many a day what my feelings are for you; so I won't
say anything more than that the one object of the
years I may have to live will be to make you happy.
I am not such a fool as to expect your feelings to
be the same as mine; but if you think you can look
upon me as a true friend now, you will, perhaps,
some day be able to get reconciled to the idea of
looking upon me in the light of a husband besides."

These were the few short sentences in which
Lord Devereux decided upon all his future life. Far
cleverer men than he ever was might have wrecked
their chance by a display of greater eloquence and
greater passion. Mildred answered after but a moment's hesitation:

"Lord Devereux, you have spoken to me frankly
and straightforwardly: I will try to answer you in the
same spirit. I suppose I ought to feign surprise at
the question you have asked me; I do not, for I did
think for some time back that you cared for me.
I believe the right thing to say is that I am flattered;
at any rate, I will say this much—that I believe lots
of girls, far prettier and more attractive than myself,
would not only answer your question in the affirmative, but would give you (you see I take you at your
word and treat you as a friend) what is not in my
power to give. I don't mind telling you—in fact, I
am bound to do so—that there is another man whose
image stands in the way of my saying Yes. I dare
say you know who it is, and also that there is no
sort of chance of my ever marrying him; but, in fairness to you, and thinking chiefly of your happiness,
I am obliged to tell you that I cannot give you the
feelings that a wife ought to have for the man she
marries for better, for worse. Don't think me harsh
or cruel; I should be cruel were my answer different."

Lord Devereux was far too wary not to have
been fully prepared for the reply that had just met
his ear; in fact, he would have been almost disappointed had his proposal been accepted then and

there. So, by no means disconcerted, he proceeded thus:

"My dear child, of course I have known all this. I know the man you mean, and a nicer fellow than he is I have seldom come across; but, as you say yourself, there is nothing to look forward to, is there? I know George Mansfield too well to think him capable of wishing you to spend your days a homeless, lonely orphan on his account. Years will roll by; you are nothing but a child, you have lost sight of him, perhaps for years; put it before him—would he not sooner himself that you should marry a man of my age, who will be more of a father to you than a husband, than that some day he should be forgotten, and the love you now feel for him should be given wholly and entirely to some other man? You see I don't expect very much, I am very humble in my pretensions; but I do honestly think I could make you fairly happy. I don't wish for a final answer; I won't listen to one even. Think it over, and tell me what you have decided a few weeks hence. Is that a bargain? And now we won't talk any more about it. What a charming voice Mrs. Garrard has!"

That lady had just sat down to the piano, with none of the fuss too many amateurs and professionals are apt to make on these occasions, and in her rich contralto voice had begun one of Moore's Irish Melodies. The conversation ceased as if by magic, and Mildred listened in rapturous silence, the tears coming to her eyes.

Whatever troubles may be weighing upon the mind—the remark does not apply to acute *bodily* suffering, as martyrs to gout would certify—it is difficult to see only the gloomy side of life when, on awaking, the sun is seen pouring in brightly, gradually dispelling the early mist, and when, as the good old hunting song has it, "All nature looks smiling and gay"; and though Mildred might feel no less worried and perplexed than she had the evening before, she could not resist the exhilarating effect of her surroundings when she appeared at breakfast calm and composed. No one had noticed anything the evening before, so she had not to pass through the ordeal of those rather impertinent, scrutinising glances that are sometimes exchanged across a breakfast table. Most of the men were on the point of leaving when she appeared downstairs, as an outlying covert had to be shot over that morning, and soon afterwards Mrs. Arthur announced her intention of driving Lady Wharnhill and Mrs. Ryder to a Primrose meeting at the neighbouring town. These arrangements thoroughly coincided with Mildred's wishes, as they offered her an opportunity of unburdening her mind of the events of the preceding evening towards the one person whom she still considered to be entitled to be taken into her confidence. As the last carriage vanished in the distance she sat down at Mrs. Arthur's smart marqueterie writing table to pen the following epistle:

My DEAR GEORGE,—By the way, I don't know why I still go on addressing you in this manner; still, I won't make any alteration to-day.

My object in writing this is to tell you that your anticipations have been verified, and that last night "old Devereux," as you call him, asked me to be his wife.

I must say he was particularly nice about it and showed a remarkable amount of tact, etc.

I could not help feeling just a little sorry for him (does that sound a very conceited speech?) for somehow he seems so terribly in earnest. He knows all about you and me, and feels dreadfully remorseful about having told you to back his horse at Ascot.

Now I wonder if you are at all curious to know what I answered; are you?

Well, of course I told him that I still cared for you and was likely to continue doing so, which naturally meant "No"; but he is one of those extraordinary men who won't take "No" for an answer, so that I daresay I shall be called upon to hear the question repeated before very long; in fact, he begged me to allow him not to look upon this as a final decision.

Now I have told you all, and I suppose I must not take up any more of your time, which belongs to those Polish recruits of yours. Have you taught them to ride bareback by now, and have they learnt how to spell your name?

I am leaving this in a day or two. Mrs. Jack does not know I am writing to you, or I have no doubt she would send you any amount of tender messages.

Yours ever,

M. C.

She had hardly finished her letter before hurried footsteps were heard outside the door, and the pretty Miss Ryder burst in, faultlessly attired as she always was and looking the picture of youth, health and prosperity.

"Oh, Mildred! we must be off, for the men will be so cross if we keep them waiting. Are you nearly ready? Do you like this hat? I was not sure whether I had not better, perhaps, put on a stalking cap."

Mildred did not seem to consider the question a very weighty one: so she did no more than assure Miss Ryder that she could not possibly look nicer than she did already; and, noticing on the other's face a genuine look of anxiety to get away, she hurriedly ran upstairs and was soon ready to join the party already seated in the waggonette.

The rest of the day and evening seemed rather long to all; and were it not for her sincere regret at parting from Mrs. Garrard, she was perhaps not sorry that the end of the week had arrived. Before parting from her new friend—whom she had soon learnt to call by her pet-name of "Maggie," under which she was known to all her friends—they promised to write as soon as they got home, and Mildred even made a half engagement to pay Mrs. Garrard a short visit once the hunting season had begun.

———

CHAPTER VII.

"Adversity hurts none, but only such
Whom whitest fortune dandled has too much."
R. HERRICK.

THE Calais boat was dancing merrily when George Mansfield descended the steps off Dover pier with a heavy heart, but one not likely to be affected by the complaint which a stiff south-westerly breeze soon produced in most of his fellow-passengers, and which the French language so strangely—and from a physiological view apparently most incorrectly—connects with the human heart. He had decided to go straight through to Vienna, so as not to waste any time; feeling, as he did, that before he could be expected to do work of any kind whatever, he must first find out what would be expected of him. During the last few months he had been pretty busy learning German, and was now fairly fluent in that language. He felt sure of meeting one friend at the end of his journey—a former brother-officer of his in the Guards, recently appointed Military Attaché in Vienna, with whom he had been frequently corresponding of late. To him he betook himself the morning after his arrival, and rattling over the huge blocks of granite with which the Vienna streets are paved, at the rate of quite ten miles an hour, he found himself at Colonel Greville's door in an incredibly short space of time.

That officer had just completed his somewhat elaborate toilet when George burst in unannounced, greeting him with the exclamations: "How are you, old chap? I say, what makes these cabs drive such a pace here? Upon my soul, they would run any of our fire-engines pretty close!"

"I suppose because the fellows inside are so hard-worked," answers the other imperturbably, but with a mildly sarcastic intonation; "they cannot afford to waste any time. But never mind about the cabs; stay and have some breakfast with me, and we will have a good long jaw."

This George Mansfield willingly assented to, anxious to find out to the best of his ability how the land lay and when he would be able to enter upon his new duties.

"As a matter of fact, my dear fellow"—these were his former brother-officer's opening words— "you have been uncommonly lucky; they have appointed you to a really crack regiment, quartered only about two hours' rail from Vienna. Your colonel is one of the finest fellows in the Army, and has seen a lot of active service. Besides, from what I hear, he has received instructions to make your life as pleasant as circumstances permit. Of course, everything in this world is relative, and a Hungarian village is not the exact counterpart of Windsor. There are no end of nice fellows in the regiment,

and I have no doubt you will soon feel quite at home;
but take my advice and discard all notions of life in
the Guards and all that sort of thing. You will
have a fairish amount of roughing it and any amount
of hard work; in fact, you will be at it all day, from
seven A.M. to five P.M., and may think yourself uncommonly lucky if your colonel allows you to go up
to Vienna every other Sunday. The men, from what
I hear, are perhaps a bit slow at first—rough sort of
devils, but uncommonly fine soldiers for all that;
and how they manage to turn them out with their
three years' system the way they do beats me altogether. I suppose you don't want to stay in Vienna
longer than just the time required to get your kit,
and then I will take you down to your regiment, and
will introduce you to the colonel. And after that,
my dear boy, you must swim for yourself."

The next few days were devoted to a certain
number of indispensable official visits, and to the
ordering of his uniforms; but before the week was
over George Mansfield found himself in a comfortable railway carriage, with his friend Colonel Greville,
steaming off for his new destination, where, for all he
knew, the rest of his life might be spent.

For the first hour or so the scenery was lovely,
beginning with a general panorama of Vienna, situated
in almost unique picturesqueness at the foot of two
lofty, vine clad mountains, with the Danube, or rather
a branch of it, winding its way right through the
heart of the city. When the lofty spire of St. Stephen
gradually vanished in the mist a range of hills became

perceptible, skirting the railway line, the summits of them girt with ruins of old feudal mansions, remnants of many a hard-fought battle in days gone by, their stern old battlements frowning upon the valley lying underneath covered with villas, hotels, cafés, and all the other attributes of modern watering-places.

Then, again, another change ensued, as rapidly as the shifting of the scenery at a play. The mountains receded more and more, and the wide plain of Hungary opened up its apparently endless stretch. A dull, dreary, monotonous steppe it may perchance seem to those who see it for the first time.

And yet there is an indescribable fascination in these Pannonian plains, comparable only to that of the Roman Campagna, which may well justify the old adage of the Magyars:

Extra Hungariam non est vita,
Si est vita, non est ita.

When examined more closely the apparent monotony will soon vanish; what seemed an unbroken surface like that of a billiard table will become animated with quaint little villages resplendent with the dazzle of their whitewashed houses, resonant with the singularly passionate and heart-stirring notes of the national tunes of which many of the Hungarian bands we hear in London ball-rooms give us but so faint a notion.

Now and then will emerge on the horizon the outline of massive castles, the ancestral seats of the old nobility, with their huge deep yellow frontage, interrupted by an almost incalculable number of green-shuttered windows: surrounded by hundreds of acres of a park, laid out in days gone by to rival more than to imitate the splendours of Versailles.

Many of these old country seats are gradually crumbling away; grass is growing thickly in those court-yards that have seen many a time the chariots of royal visitors drive up to their doors; the gloomy sound of the owl, and other birds of the night, is heard along those vast terraces trodden by many a dainty foot in olden days, and the bats are making merry along the endless passages that used to resound with the clash of sword and scabbard.

"Here we are, old chap," are the words by which George Mansfield is aroused out of his reverie, for upon him the scenery had not failed to produce the effect it generally does at first sight—that of intense depression; "this is Toronya, where the regiment is quartered—at least one troop of it is, for the rest are scattered all about the neighbourhood, and I don't exactly know to which of these villages they will send you. Anyhow, we will have some breakfast, and then we will go and see the Colonel. After that I suppose you will be sworn in, so we can then rig you out in your new kit, and after that I will say good-bye, as I must get back to dine out to-night."

It may not be generally known that the Austrian cavalry all over the Dual Monarchy is permanently billeted out, even in time of peace, only some few of the largest cities having recently constructed barracks for the mounted troops.

The staffs of the regiments are mostly located in the more important centres of the different provinces, and the regiment itself will be scattered within a radius varying from two to ten miles. The four troops of each of the six squadrons are clustered round the localities where the Escadrons-Commandant (squadron-leader) is quartered; but in time of peace each troop, consisting of about thirty-five men and as many horses, practically forms a unit of its own.

Occasionally a sergeant-major is left in command of a troop, but the usual practice is that a lieutenant or sub-lieutenant should be what is called Zugs-Commandant (troop-leader), and as such he will in all probability pass his days, as only officer in a little village or hamlet, with his handful of men. At what distance he may be from any of his brother-officers of course varies very much, according to the density of the population and the number of human dwellings in the different provinces. As a rule, it will not exceed two or three miles; but, bearing in mind that during the winter months communication by the little lanes connecting the various villages becomes at times all but impossible, a distance of three miles constitutes as effective a barrier as one of thirty.

This system has been in existence almost since time immemorial, and has been kept up partly from reasons of economy, but chiefly from the exceedingly satisfactory results obtained by it.

Amongst these may be mentioned the far more intimate knowledge of their men acquired by the officers through being much more frequently brought

into contact with them, and the early development
of that stern sense of duty, and chiefly of responsibility,
which is naturally roused by the far greater scope
that is granted to a young officer within a year or
two of his joining.

As a matter of fact, a sub-lieutenant is a far
more important personage in an Austrian cavalry
regiment than a captain with us, as he is solely
responsible for the efficiency of his troop. Moreover,
the training of the recruits, a certain number of whom
is told off to every troop in the regiment, devolves
upon him; and if he enjoys the full confidence of his
captain he may be entrusted with the breaking-in of
some of the remounts.

In any unforeseen emergency such as a fire—a
most frequent occurrence in Hungarian villages, where
almost all the houses are roofed with thatch—or in
the eventuality of any disturbance between his men
and the peasant population—an incident which, not
unusual in former days, is now exceedingly rare—he
has no one to consult but himself, though, of course,
he will subsequently report to his captain the steps
he has taken on every separate occasion.

Thus a comparatively very large sphere of activity
is given to a young fellow who, stimulated by a
healthy spirit of emulation, will spare no trouble to
make his troop the smartest of the squadron—or of
the regiment, if he can—knowing that any *kudos*
thus obtained will fall entirely upon him.

No doubt the life is a stern and somewhat austere
one, doubly so from the fact of the promotion being

slow. On the other hand, the system has so
familiarised itself with the growth of successive
generations that it is looked upon quite as a matter
of course.

Heirs to proud titles and large fortunes are quite
happy to do as their fathers and grandfathers have
done before them, and take naturally to a life which
does not even strike them as one of great hardship
or privation, trusting to the monotony of routine
being relieved by the unbounded hospitality of whatever country houses there may be in the neighbourhood, by a fair amount of shooting and, possibly, in
some favoured districts, a gallop with harriers.

During the summer months each regiment in turn
marches off to the manœuvres; and it is only on the
first of October of every year that the work in the
riding-school is resumed with every successive batch
of recruits.

A large additional amount of work obviously
devolves upon the regimental officers in consequence
of the short service system, and the resulting difficulty of keeping the non-commissioned officers with
the colours after their three years have expired.

Ten minutes' drive through the ill-paved streets
of the straggling town of Toronya, where the staff of
the 24th Lancers was quartered, brought George and
his friend to the chief hotel of the place, where
luncheon was soon served. A few glasses of generous
old Hungarian wine, that makes every pulse quicken
and dispels care—as its name of "Sorgenbrecher" is
intended to convey—soon brings George back to his

wonted spirits; and his one wish now is to get over all the preliminaries, and set to work at once.

After luncheon, he is taken by his friend to pay a visit to Count Wartenstein, the Colonel of the regiment. A tall, dark man, of soldierly bearing, clad in the undress uniform of his regiment, rises to meet them, and shakes hands cordially with both. The expression of the very high-bred features is a serious, almost a sad one, and is not very frequently lighted up by a smile from underneath the black, curled moustache. And yet, if all tales are true, Colonel Wartenstein has had more than his share of the good things of life. Every favour has been showered upon him; his promotion has been a rapid one; and that voice that rings out the word of command in tones as clear as those of a silver bugle, has, when dropping to softer notes, set many heart-strings stirring.

His clear brown eyes settle somewhat fixedly upon George, whose arrival in the regiment is rather an unusual occurrence; so the Colonel means to have a good look at his new officer. He is pleased at the imperturbable manner in which George bears his scrutinising glance, and he continues with a little more warmth:

"I need hardly say I am very glad you have been gazetted to my regiment. We used in former days to have many foreigners in our service; but that is a thing of the past; as a matter of fact, we don't encourage them to come as a rule. Of course, it will take you some little time before you get to know our work, and for the next two or three months you won't be able to do much more than look on; still, you can be very useful even now with the remounts. I have told you off to Prince Saalburg's squadron, the 6th, at Zsadany, and I have particularly recommended him to give you every opportunity of learning your work as quickly as possible, as I should like to put you in command of a troop before very long."

After a few remarks as to a short stay he had made in England some years back, and to the sport he had seen when hunting in the Pytchley country, the interview came to an end. Then, after taking an affectionate leave of his friend and thanking him for his assistance, George Mansfield, having duly taken the oath, hurried back to his hotel and spent the next half-hour coping successfully with his new uniform, in which he was now to spend the greater part of his life; for, according to Austrian Army regulations, the uniform is worn on and off duty. He now felt that the final step had been taken, and he was determined to make the best of his new life. It was too late to start the same evening for the village of Zsadany, which was to be his final destination; so he made up his mind to a solitary evening, devoted chiefly to his somewhat neglected correspondence.

CHAPTER VIII.

"Der Soldat hat auf Erden kein bleibend Quartier,
Kann treue Lieb' nicht bewahren."

SCHILLER.

EARLY next morning, the new subaltern set out in one of the native conveyances, drawn by two *Juckers* that thought themselves aggrieved when not allowed to travel at the rate of quite ten miles an hour. Not many minutes' drive took him outside the gates of the town; and a perfectly straight high-road, running along on a dead level, opened up to the eye for a distance that, owing to the extreme clearness and transparency of the atmosphere, seemed almost endless. Rich pasture land lay to either side of the road, interrupted only an occasional clump of trees, but without any sort of enclosure; and frequently the driver would leave the dusty, stony high-road and indulge in a spin over the springy turf. "Nice country, this, to handle cavalry," thought George; "no wonder they quarter them out here; their horses ought to be pretty fit, anyhow."

He was too busy taking in every detail of a country in which everything was strange to him to notice the time passing by, and was almost surprised when his driver, booted and spurred like his com-

patriots of that class almost invariably are, pointed
with his whip to a white steeple on a slight elevation
about half-a-mile off, and informed his passenger that
that was Zsadany. George's interest increased, the
nearer he approached his destination, and was
at its height when he entered a village apparently
consisting merely of a double row of whitewashed,
one-storied houses, with mostly not more than one
window to the front but receding to some depth
at the back. Open-mouthed, ragged children stared
at him with some amazement, and numberless street-
curs holding their siesta in the middle of the road
yapped and snarled angrily as his carriage rattled by.

Meeting one or two privates loitering about, he
inquired where the captain's quarters were. The
answer was given in a tone of intense surprise that
anybody should ignore the residence of a personage
who, to those addressed, was invested with almost
supernatural attributes. However, they showed him
to a building lying some fifty yards off the main
road, in the centre of a vast farmyard. The building itself was of larger dimensions than the other
houses George had seen, but in no other way dis-
similar.

Having ascertained that Captain Prince Saalburg
was at home, George was duly shown in and began
by officially reporting himself as having been gazetted to the 6th Squadron. During the fifty seconds
that this formality lasted he felt his captain's eye
looking him over from top to toe; for a very mar-
tinet he was on duty, and nothing escaped his quick

glance. Before the last word had passed his lips
the professionally stern look left Prince Saalburg's
countenance, and he greeted George with an almost
boisterous welcome.

The heir to an historical name and a large property, he had made the army his profession and
loved it with all his heart and soul. The knowledge
that his squadron was, perhaps, the best turned out
in the whole cavalry gave him far more pleasure
than any sort of gratification that his position and
wealth could have enabled him to command. Though
a keen sportsman, he seldom went on leave, and
never for long; and the fascinations of the fair sex
could never wile him away for any time from his incessant pre-occupation for the efficiency and the
welfare of his squadron. He was the terror of his
young subalterns, for he would pounce down upon
them in their outlying villages when least expected;
and woe betide them if a curb-chain was found too
tight, or a pair of stirrup-leathers not the exact regulation length.

"None of your young fellows for me," he was
wont to say, "who want to go up to town every
week and join the regiment, because they think it is
a smart thing to do! If a man is a soldier, he cannot be anything else and do the two things properly."

During half-an-hour's talk, George was gradually
being initiated into the rudiments of what his new
professional life was going to be. The winter months
were devoted almost exclusively to the drilling of

the recruits who were to join on the 1st of October. By the 1st of May they must take their place in the ranks and cease to be considered recruits. "Pretty quick work, isn't it?" added the Captain. "Of course we only keep them three years; so we dare not lose any time. We don't profess to turn them out quite like your Lifeguardsmen; we did in the old days when we kept them eight or nine years; but, such as you see them now, for real work I will back them against any cavalry in the world. And now I'll come round with you to your quarters; and then we will go to have some dinner."

The surprised look in George's face set him off into peals of merry laughter: "You must not mind that; we always dine at twelve or twelve-thirty, and then we have some tea or something in the evening."

Upon this unexpected statement George made the internal reflection that any misgivings he might have had of late as to increasing in weight were now likely to prove unnecessary; but he was determined to see the bright side of everything, and only said to himself that if all these fellows could do it, he presumably could too. He thereupon followed his Captain into the street. About a hundred yards off the latter stopped and said:

"This is where you are going to live; it is the best place we could find, and it has always been the officers' quarters. Mind the door; it is rather low."

George was now ushered into a room about twenty-four feet by eighteen. Heavy rafters ran

across the wooden ceiling; the walls were whitewashed, and the floor consisted of plain deals. An
enormous stove, or rather oven, of bright green tiles,
reaching nearly to the ceiling and with a wooden
bench running around it, was the first and rather
unfamiliar object that met his eye. In the further
end of the room stood a bedstead, with many-
coloured quilts—the only luxury the Hungarian
peasant allows himself—piled upon each other. A
deal table and a chair or two completed the furniture.
George had made up his mind to appear surprised
at nothing; so he only said:

"That will do very nicely. I shall have my
own things coming out from England before very
long. Anyhow, I think I will have the window
open a bit; that feather bed makes the place rather
stuffy."

Prince Saalburg was slightly disappointed; for
he had expected some loud manifestation of surprise,
possibly disgust; but inwardly he was beginning to
feel some respect for his new subaltern.

"You must try and make yourself understood as
best you can with your soldier servant; like most of
our men, he speaks nothing but Polish; but he is
sharp enough, and it will be a capital opportunity
for you to learn the language. In three months you
ought to be able to make yourself fairly well understood by the men. And now let us go to dinner."

The little inn where this early meal was to take
place lay on the high road at the farther end of the
village; its appearance was not prepossessing. Two

or three carters making their mid-day halt and a few
itinerant pedlars sat in the public room replete with
smoke and the smell of burnt grease. Beyond this
lay the room reserved for the use of the officers.
George noticed that every occupant of the public
room jumped to his feet at the sight of the "Herr
Rittmeister" (Captain), and saluted him with the
deepest of bows.

"This is where we shall dine together every day
for the next three months," said the latter. "You
will see that the cooking is not bad, although there
is not very much variety; but, on the other hand it
is not expensive; we pay eighteen florins (thirty
shillings) a month."

This last statement fairly took George's breath
away. "A month, do you say?" and to himself:
"By Jove, the bookies at home ought to thank Providence that sent me here!"

"Yes, I suppose it does seem little," said the
other; "I dare say you used often to spend more
than that on one dinner. But then we don't eat very
much; for at two o'clock we have to be at the riding
school again. They have sent us a larger number
of remounts than usual this year, and they are still
very backward; so we have to be busy with them all
the afternoon; and the days are getting so short!
Would you like to try your hand at riding some of
them to-day? You have plenty of time to change
your things between this and two."

"You are the right sort for me!" thought George,
and he willingly assented.

On returning to his quarters, which he had some
little trouble in finding, from the exact similarity of
all the houses, he found his servant putting barrow-
loads of fuel into the stove through an opening it
had from the passage outside; for its surface towards
the room was innocent of any aperture. The man
promptly emerged from out of the stove and addressed George with some volubility, apparently asking for orders.

"All right, my man!" said George; "I have not
a notion what you are saying, but you don't look a
fool; and I dare say we shall get on very nicely together."

Not many minutes later he was jogging round
an open-air riding school, with a keen east wind
raising up clouds of dust, on an unbroken colt with
only one side to its mouth, seated in a regulation
saddle which, though believed to be the very acme
of comfort in its downward action, is no doubt constructed with a view to that. This went on for
about a couple of hours, George having ridden suc-
cessively four or five remounts to his captain's entire
satisfaction.

"That will do for to-day," said the latter at
last; and he ordered the horses to be taken back.
"We will now look in at the men's school on our
way home."

Darkness was setting in before the routine work
of the day had come to an end. Nevertheless George
had learnt this much on the first day of his arrival,
that if he were to feel discontented with his new life

it would not be from want of occupation. He had not been able to gather much information as yet from Prince Saalburg with regard to any social resources the neighbourhood might possess. The latter had casually referred to a country house about five miles off where he sometimes went for the evening; "but not often," he added. "I like my quiet evenings at home; it is the only time I have for reading, and I am now very busy writing an essay on cavalry tactics. On Saturdays I generally ride in to headquarters and spend Sunday there. I hope next time you will come in with me, and you will get to know all your brother officers."

Thereupon they parted, and George betook himself to his quarters, wondering what he would do with himself throughout the evening, all the more as dinner was a thing of the past and he was entirely dependent upon the wits of his soldier servant for any subsequent meal that might be produced. The latter, however, was not taken at a loss and even managed to display a slight smattering of culinary knowledge. Nevertheless the meal was primitive enough, and George could not help smiling inwardly at the idea of what the inmates of the servants' hall at his brother's place would say if exposed to the indignity of having such humble fare placed before them.

As the clock on the steeple struck eight, the long-drawn, weird notes of the bugle-call for the *retraite* (equivalent to our "tattoo") resounded throughout the village, and a few minutes afterwards not a sound was to be heard but the occasional angry bark of a street dog. Everything outside was in absolute darkness; the east wind had freshened since the afternoon and was driving the rain and the sleet in great gusts against the window panes. It must be said to poor George's credit that he kept up his spirits manfully. Picking out the least straight-backed of the two chairs that were at his disposal, he settled himself down, had a good pull at his flask, lit a pipe and began to think.

"Wednesday; why, of course, it was the day of the St. Leger." He wondered what had won, and when he was likely to hear of it. Eight o'clock; people just beginning to think about dinner; how different things looked at that time last year. He smiled at the recollection of what a cheery party it had been; every incident, even the most trifling one, seemed to come back to him. "I wonder," he said, thinking aloud, "if anybody at Doncaster has even noticed I wasn't there to-day; I don't suppose they did. It could not do me much good, either, if they had. It is a funny world! Am I now going to spend all my evenings like this for the next years to come, between a petroleum lamp and the carcass of a consumptive chicken? If I do, I will make myself a bit more comfortable. I wonder what Mildred is doing now." His face saddens, and pensively he watches the coils of smoke as they slowly rise. "The whole thing was awfully hard on her, poor child; and the thought of her alone ought to have kept me straight. Anyhow, I have made whatever amends I could. I suppose eventually she will follow my advice and will marry old Devereux; that will make a nice cheery day for me out here, her wedding-day will." He brings down his heel with a rattle that elicits an angry bark from David, his old fox-terrier, who had followed him into his new life. At any rate, it was no good thinking of all that now; "sufficient unto the day," etc., and soon after he devoted himself to the composition of a long letter to the young lady whose vision was before his mind. He gave her a minute account of all he had seen and done during the last few days, followed up by a very cheery sketch of what he anticipated his new life would be. He wound up thus:

Of course it is a totally different thing from soldiering at home; but, from the little I have seen, I feel sure I shall take to it; so far everybody has been most kind to me, so don't you make yourself unhappy about me.

Send me every book you can think of; not only novels but something that will improve my mind; I am sure it must be in want of it, and I shall have plenty of leisure for reading in the evening.

For how long I may be out here nobody can tell. My first duty is to pay up as soon as ever I can; I shall not be happy until that is done.

Don't fret about me, for I shall get on all right. Don't be too unselfish, and try to think more about yourself than about   Your very devoted

G. M.

Soon afterwards he dismantled the structure of feather beds and before long was sleeping the sleep of the just.

*   *   *   *   *

Days followed each other. George Mansfield's indefatigable love of work, coupled with his genial, cheery manner, soon won him the affection of his superiors, who spoke most highly of him. He had gradually made the acquaintance of all his different brother officers during his occasional visits to head-quarters and soon felt thoroughly at home amongst them, never finding anything but the utmost cordiality and the same free and easy manner to which he was accustomed in his old regiment.

After three or four months of hard work he was considered to have made sufficient progress to be put in command of a troop, quartered a few miles off, which meant absolute solitude instead of Prince Saalburg's company, with whom he had quite made friends. Their meetings would now be comparatively rare, chiefly dependent upon the requirements of the service.

Nevertheless, in many respects the change meant an improvement to him. To begin with, he was far more his own master, instead of merely carrying out his captain's orders; and on the other hand, he soon gathered that at his new quarters he would be within about a couple of miles from the country seat of a family, one member of which he had once met in England—a fact which would help to facilitate an introduction.

The Counts of Szent Imre were amongst the largest landowners in Hungary, and the castle of Kisfalva only one of the many country houses inhabited by them in turn. The old castle, which in the days of Turkish invasions had withstood many a hard siege, formed rather a prominent feature in the landscape around, situated on a slight elevation and surrounded by miles of park and deer forest. A long avenue of poplars led up to the drawbridge that gave access to the outer court, from which the main building, looking rather like an ancient fortress, with its old turrets and battlements, was soon reached.

From his conversation with various of his brother officers, George had gathered that Countess Szent Imre appeared to be the reigning beauty of the neighbourhood, and that he ought to think himself lucky at being quartered within such easy reach of Kisfalva. He thought he noticed a few significant glances being exchanged around him on this subject, and his curiosity was beginning to be aroused.

Soon after George Mansfield had joined, his two chargers and a useful, fast-trotting cob had arrived. With the aid of a few bits of comfortable furniture, a large collection of sporting prints, etc., his one solitary room was gradually taking a more inhabitable appearance. Looking back in after years upon the many lonely evenings he had spent with no other company than that of his books, of which he was collecting a steadily increasing stock, he felt inclined to wonder why the recollection of them was not by any means an unpleasant one. Winter had now set

in in real earnest. Frequently, for several consecutiv
days, the little cottage he lived in would be almost
buried in snow, great drifts blocking up the roads
and all but cutting off the village from the outside
world. A narrow path had been dug up between
his house and the inn where he went for his meal
that was styled by the euphonious name of dinner,
and which mostly consisted of rather greasy soup,
boiled beef and a rice pudding.

CHAPTER IX.

"Love in her sunny eyes doth basking play,
    Love walks the pleasant mazes of her hair;
Love doth on both her lips for ever stray,
    And sows and reaps a thousand kisses there."
                                    ABRAHAM COWLEY.

TOWARDS the middle of January George received
a message from one of his brother officers that
Count and Countess Szent Imre would be glad to
see him any day he liked to call at Kisfalva, even
without the formality of an introduction; so he had
the cob—who was getting rather above himself for
want of work—put to a narrow and very low sleigh
he had bought in the neighbouring town, and set off
for his wintry drive, well provided with the thickest
gloves and a fur bag, in which all the lower part of
his person was buried.

The view, once he had left the village behind,
was striking enough. The air was absolutely still
and the sun shining brightly. As far as the eye
could reach not a living being nor any landmark of
any kind was to be seen; all traffic on wheels had
been suspended for some time, and there was scarcely
any indication as to where the road lay.

As he went skimming along over the hard-frozen
snow, he noticed, before he had gone very far, a

figure which he thought he identified as that of the parish priest of the village he was quartered in. He slackened as he was about to pass him, and inquired whether he could be of any use, as he had plenty of room in his sledge. The gratified expression that lighted up the thin, pale face of the monk, went straight to George's heart; and, making room for him, he asked what errand might have brought him away from home on a day like that, and so insufficiently protected against the inclemency of the climate.

"I should not have minded the weather so much, Herr Lieutenant," was the answer, "and I should have walked the five miles to Csernova and back willingly, only I was so afraid of getting there too late. There is a poor old man dying rapidly, who has no one to look after him, and there is no priest nearer than myself. Poor old Janko! he would not hear of us when he was well and strong, and went poaching amongst the Kisfalva preserves, and came home tipsy every Sunday afternoon: but now he has sent for me, and bade me not lose a minute. How fast your horse goes! But perhaps you are not going as far as Csernova?"

"Oh! he can go a lot faster than that," said George—and to the cob; "Come on, old man. No, I was going to Kisfalva, but now that you have told me what your errand is, your old poacher shall not die with no one to comfort him, if I can help it."

The poor priest's gratitude was expressed warmly, though with no sort of effusion; but the earnest look

from the expressive eyes that lighted up an otherwise plain countenance spoke volumes.

"You have not been at Erdelyi long, have you,
Herr Lieutenant? At least, I have never seen you"
—he was going to say "in church," but, colouring
deeply, he stopped short—"excepting once or twice
at the riding-school."

"No, Hochwürden." (It is thus the Catholic
clergy are universally addressed in Austria and
Hungary.) "I have only been here a few weeks. I
am afraid I have not come in for the best time of
year. But don't you find it very dull yourself,
too?"

"No, I cannot say I do; in fact, a little time ago
I was offered a large parish at Buda-Pest, but I did
not care to go. Besides, my little flock objected to
my leaving. I am very much attached to them; I
wish I was able to do more. No, I long to remain
here. At Buda-Pest I should not have time to read,
and I feel I can be almost of more use in a little
place like this. But it must be dull indeed for
you."

The shy and rather nervous manner of his companion did not facilitate George's conversational
efforts; and though he inwardly felt there was more
in the man than met the eye, he was not sorry to
have pointed out to him a little detached farmhouse
on the roadside as the priest's destination. On the
latter's assurance that there was no probability of
his being able to return home that evening, they
parted, as George could not but realise that his pre-

sence at the bedside of the old poacher would be more than superfluous.

Turning his pony's head in the direction whence he had come, he decided to carry out his original intention of calling upon Countess Szent Imre.

As the stern old battlements of the Castle of Kisfalva became more plainly discernible, when the snow sent up by the pony's hind feet, as from a catapult, did not shut off the view altogether, George could not resist a certain feeling of curiosity concerning the lady to whom his visit was destined.

Having emerged from his fur wraps and brushed off the snow that lay thick upon his hair and moustache, he was shown into a boudoir where he was told the Countess would shortly join him. Twilight was beginning to set in, and the room was chiefly lighted by the reflection of the flames that danced and flickered merrily around the heavy oak logs in the grate.

A passing glance sufficed to show that this room must evidently be the favourite nook of a person of exceedingly refined taste. It bore in every one of its details the distinct stamp of the individuality of the owner, from a Greuze of no common merit on the panel facing the entrance down to a Louis XIV. vitrine, containing some choice pieces of Sèvres china. Every object that caught the eye was plainly indicative of careful selection. A chaise-longue, likewise of the period of the "Roi Soleil," stood out at an angle to the fire-place, within easy reach of a small and curiously-worked gilt bookcase. On an easel at

the head of the writing-table George noticed a pastel
portrait, at which he was gazing with rapt attention
when the door was thrown open to admit the original
of the portrait.

Slightly above the middle height, with a figure
remarkable for its flexibility and the exquisite gracefulness of all its movements, with hands and feet
that fully deserved the sonnet with which they once
inspired an amorous compatriot of hers addicted to
lyrics, the Countess of Szent Imre might well be described, even by the most fastidious judge, as well
worthy of her reputation of a singularly lovely
woman.

Possibly her features might not in every point
come up to the standard of one who judges feminine
beauty solely by the outlines that Phidias and Praxi-
teles have immortalised. A captious critic might
possibly object to the eyes being placed rather closer
together than the laws of faultless symmetry would
rule, or to an almost imperceptible upward curve in
the outline of the nose; but, having said that much,
he would fain subside into a respectful and admiring
silence.

Her face was an almost faultless oval, and the
general expression of the features one of all but in-
describle softness and charm. Under the delicately
pencilled brows and under the shadow of long, curly
eyelashes shone a pair of green eyes that few men
would gaze at dispassionately. Their usual expression was one of intense indolence and indifference;
but trust them not! They may at any moment

awaken to an almost childlike look of surprise, of
sympathy, of interest. They will flash forth sparks
of lightning when aroused to anger; they have been
seen half-veiled by the delicate drooping lids, as if
for fear their glorious lustre might betray their un-
resisting acquiescence with the fervid, impassioned
words of love they had inspired.

The complexion is a singularly delicate one, and
the generous blood of a Southern race is seen running through the network of fine blue veins perceptible on the clear white brow and temples.

The low tones of a rich contralto voice greet
George as she steps into the room with the graceful,
undulating motion that stamps a thorough-bred woman. She addresses him in his own language, with
a barely noticeable foreign accent:

"I am so glad, Lord George, that you have at
last made up your mind to emerge from your solitude. We were all wondering what the attractions
of Erdelyi could be that had prevented you from
calling here before. I believe I met your brother
some years ago in London; isn't he rather a grave
man, with a beard, who takes an interest in
Church matters and philanthropy and that sort of
thing?"

George at once expressed his recognition of
Lord Errington from the above description, and conversation soon flowed along easily and smoothly.
His surprise was great at finding his fair companion
well acquainted with every branch of modern litera-
ture, as well as with the last topic of London gossip;

full of originality and a delightful disregard of conventionalism.

Time passed; and when George bid farewell to his hostess he was surprised to see how late it was; and he wondered inwardly how he would ever get home again.

"Now that you have found your way to Kisfalva," said Countess Szent Imre before parting, "I hope you will not forget it. My husband has been very delicate of late, so we are not having anybody to stay with us, but I hope you will come and propose yourself to dinner whenever it is convenient to you."

An icy blast met George as he left this hospitable mansion, and his drive back over the hard-frozen road, with his pony pulling double, brought him back to stern reality and the prospects of a solitary evening.

The postal communication, interrupted for several days owing to the heavy fall of snow, had been restored; so George found an accumulated budget of news contained in quite a pile of letters.

To the dweller in busy London, reading a letter, answering and forgetting it, is often the work of not more than five minutes; but anyone who has ever felt himself in a position at all resembling that of George Mansfield will readily understand the eagerness with which he scanned his letters one by one, sorting them into those to read the same evening and others that would keep until the morrow.

The first one to be opened was Mildred Charteris', containing the news that Lord Devereux had proposed to her. There was nothing unexpected in the news; in fact, it only verified his own predictions. Nevertheless it came to him like a severe shock. The fact that the proposal had not been accepted impressed him far less deeply than its having been made so soon after his departure.

Brooding over it in his solitary seclusion, it struck him more forcibly than ever before, that every law of honour and duty obliged him to renew the act of renunciation he had once already made. He shuddered at the responsibility he would assume in allowing any recollection of the past to influence the future of the child who had put her faith in him.

Even natures in no respect above the common may, at certain moments under the pressure of a powerful conviction, raise themselves to deeds of almost heroic self-abnegation — frequently regretted soon afterwards.

Within half-an-hour from the time he received Mildred's letter, George Mansfield had given the following missive to his servant to take at once to the neighbouring post-office:—

My DEAR MILDRED,

Owing to interruption of communications, your letter of Saturday only reached me to-day; and I answer it at once.

More than ever I feel it to be my duty to impress upon you the necessity of forgetting the past — of wiping out every recollection of it. The thought

that, but for me, your life's happiness would be in-
sured, that I have to all intents and purposes ruined
your life—is far harder for me to bear than anything else.

Every word I have written is Gospel truth; and
there is no greater happiness in store for me than to
know that if I have wronged you—unintentionally,
God knows—the harm done was not irreparable.

I cannot write more to-day. Bless you!

G. M.

With the recollection of a painful duty successfully accomplished, George Mansfield woke up next
morning to resume his every-day routine work.

At 7 a.m. he was once more busy in the riding-
school, which, by dint of straw and manure profusely
strewn about, had been made fit for use. The ten
recruits that had been told off to his troop were
progressing satisfactorily; and, as he saw them jogging round the school, keeping their seats fairly well
without reins or stirrups, he felt justified in giving
them a hearty word of encouragement.

The cold was intense, and George kept pacing
up and down the riding-school, occasionally cracking
his long whip to keep up his circulation; but he felt
on good terms with himself and the world in general
when he dismissed the last "class," and went off to
his frugal mid-day meal.

Practically, nearly every hour of his day was devoted to one or the other of his manifold duties;
and by the time he returned to his solitary quarters,

physical fatigue was mostly sufficient to prevent his
thoughts taking too wide a flight or lingering too
tenderly on the past. The difficulty of communication prevented his seeing as much of his cheery,
light-hearted brother officers as might have been desirable for him; consequently, the scant amount of
leisure he had was chiefly devoted to the company
of Countess Szent Imre and Father Vincent, the
parish priest.

Towards the latter he gradually felt himself
powerfully attracted, though in his cynical moments
he would sometimes smile grimly at what fellows at
home would say at the idea of his drinking tea with
a parson two or three nights a-week. The child-like
faith of the latter—child-like in its simplicity and
earnestness, though founded on the most extensive
knowledge of authors, ancient and modern—impressed him with a deep respect, bordering on admiration. The width of his views, free from anything
resembling exclusiveness or bigotry, was to George a
source of ever-recurring surprise, being so totally at
variance with the familiar, distorted notion of the
Catholic priest; but, above all, the utter self-abnegation with which the monk devoted himself to his
arduous duties of ministering to the wants of the
sick and the poor, showed human life under an
aspect from which it had never yet been contem-
plated by the young officer.

Once his first shyness and reserve had worn off,
George found in Father Vincent a knowledge of
human nature that fairly took him aback. Where

could a common village priest, whose life had been spent between the walls of a seminary, and the no less narrow horizon of a Hungarian village, have acquired so deep an insight into problems, the existence of which he could but know from hearsay?

With consummate tact, Father Vincent carefully avoided questioning George, even after some intimacy had been established between the two, on any merely personal matters; though he was, no doubt, able to guess from remarks casually dropped during their lengthy conversations, that the young officer's life, unlike his own, had been one disturbed by storms and passions.

The serene, placid manner of the priest had a soothing effect upon George, when, as would happen at times, visions of the past would oppress his mind as if to taunt him with his own folly, making him restless and feverishly discontented. He would often then ask himself the question whether the life of this priest, devoted exclusively to self-sacrifice and to the ministering to the wants of others—a life ignorant of ambition, passion and the search of pleasure—was not in reality a far happier one than his own had been, in which he could count on his fingers the few really unselfish actions it included. And what was this due to? Circumstances, the perversity of his nature, or what?

As long as mankind exists it will be, presumably, very much the same. "Falso queritur de natura sua genus humanum," said grim old Sallust many centuries ago; and thus it will be to the end of the chapter. Happiness exists to man born of woman only in the past or in the future.

When George found he was giving way too much to his meditative moods he would betake himself, not infrequently, to while away an hour or two with his charming country neighbour.

Countess Ilona Szent Imre was at that time in the very acme of her beauty, at that age when a woman's knowledge of the world gives her the additional subtle charm – hard to define and comparable only to the art of thought-reading—of knowing almost by intuition the exact state of a man's feelings towards her. Fully aware, though apparently never conscious of her power, she disdained, as wholly unworthy of her, the threadbare artifices of the professional coquette. The little allurements of side-glances, clasping of hands and other stage "business" of common flirtations she left to others of meaner clay, for she derived no more satisfaction from the fact of another man's falling in love with her than a crack shot does from each additional bird put down to his bag. The result was that more than one too ardent admirer had been seen leaving the old mansion of Kisfalva on anything but good terms with himself.

Coldness? A high tone of religious or moral feeling? Extreme modesty? No, indeed! The feeling that prompted her might probably be traceable to a form of self-respect that caused her to place too high a value on herself to fritter away promiscu-

ously that which she gave only in giving her whole
heart.   The beautiful lines of Schiller:

> Ich theile meine Freuden nicht; dem Einen,
> Dem Einzigen, den ich mir auserkoren,
> Geb' ich für Alles—Alles hin,

would, perhaps, best describe the secret springs of a
strangely complex nature by no means devoid of
contradictions; or, rather the nobler and vastly pre-
dominant side of it; for there was another one,
known only to herself, that might perhaps justify
some of the strictures on feminine inconsistency, accumulated during successive centuries.

A total disregard for the hollow rules of purely
conventional ethics allowed her to talk to George
about herself and her past life with the greatest
freedom.   She had married when little more than a
child, only to lose her husband after a year or two
of blissful happiness.   Left a widow before she was
twenty, she had, after some years, allowed herself to
be persuaded to marry Count Szent Imre, a remote
connection of hers.   His fortune and position made
the match a desirable one; and the difference of age
—he was past fifty at the time—dispensed her from
the obligation of professing sentiments which she
could not feel.   Her husband, at that moment a
confirmed invalid, was kindness itself towards her,
and every spring, as long as his health permitted, he
accompanied her on a visit to her numerous friends
in England.

Though, in George's mind, every link that bound
him to Mildred had been severed by his last letter,

her image was still too present in his thoughts for
him not to have carefully avoided anything in the
shape of a common flirtation; but his growing intimacy with Countess Szent Imre was of so peculiar a
kind, and could so well be covered by the elastic
term of friendship, that it was with no feeling of self-
reproach that he saw his visits to Kisfalva becoming
more and more frequent.

Confidence is rarely one-sided; and, before very
long, he had reciprocated it by communicating the
history of his life, his betrothal and the breaking of
it. During the whole of his tale, the Countess sat
motionless, her eyes fixed upon the glowing embers
in a silent reverie.

"Poor girl!" were her only words when he had
done speaking, and, after a few seconds' pause: "and
shall you be very unhappy, do you suppose, if she
does follow your advice and marry Lord Devereux?"

The question was asked in the most commonplace manner, intended merely to convey the proper
amount of interest which, in polite society, the misfortunes of our friends are expected to evoke in us.

"Yes, very unhappy!" was George's laconic
answer.

CHAPTER X.

"'Tis well to be merry and wise;
'Tis well to be honest and true;
'Tis well to be off with the old love
Before you are on with the new."

WEEKS went by. The first symptoms of Nature's revival were gradually becoming perceptible; the snow slowly disappeared, to give place to an evil far more formidable—fathomless mud. Circulation in the village of Erdelyi and in its neighbourhood became more difficult still, and had not military etiquette forbidden it, George would fain have used stilts to go to the little inn where he took his frugal mid-day meal.

At the same time, his duties absorbed even more of his time than previously. By the first of May all the recruits of his troop were to be inspected by the Colonel before taking their places in the ranks, and George was anxious to show what he had done. Truly the metamorphosis undergone by these men was sufficient for their own parents to have some difficulty in recognising them. Pale, underfed striplings, they had arrived on joining the regiment, mostly clad in a twill suit, a straw hat and innocent of anything in the shape of boots, the very use of which was unknown to many of them.

Look at them now, as they pass muster round the riding-school under George's critical eye! Square and erect they sit on their chargers, thoroughly at home in their smart uniforms, nervously anxious to carry out every injunction imparted them by their officer, whom they idolise. For George's rough and ready manner, cursing them roundly even for the smallest piece of neglect, but on the other hand never stinting them in words of approval or encouragement whenever he has an occasion to do so, has won their hearts entirely; they feel the lively and unflagging interest he takes in them and their well-being.

Six months to teach a man to dress a horse, to sit it and handle it in all its paces along the road and across a country; to clean his kit; to use his carbine; to understand his drill, mounted and unmounted, is a short allowance of time, no doubt. But as he sees the last man of the class leave the riding-school, George cannot help saying to himself, with legitimate pride, that they ought to pass muster satisfactorily even before the relentlessly critical eye of Colonel Count Wartenstein.

*   *   *   *   *

Few and far between, indeed, are the natures in which Love will resist the ordeal of prolonged separation. That this should be so —indignant protestations of enthusiastic lovers notwithstanding—is, perhaps, one of the saddest among the many sad truths concerning the inner life of mankind. It is a law of nature as unvarying and inexorable as the law of

gravitation. We may indignantly deny it—we probably, most of us, have at some period or other of
our lives; we may declare ourselves superior to the
general law, *e pur si muove.*

During the first few weeks George thought nothing of walking or riding several miles over slippery,
frozen roads to call at the nearest post-office on the
days he thought he might expect a letter from
Mildred. Almost feverishly he would watch the clerk
sorting the letters; and his face would sink at being
told, in a sympathising tone, that there was nothing
for him that day. Then, after a few weeks, the
roads would be too bad and he would wait—im-
patiently, no doubt—until the letter was delivered in
the natural course of events. When received it would
be read and re-read and put by and treasured together with its fellows. The diminution in the intensity of feeling with which each successive missive
was received, was probably almost imperceptible, but
its ratio of progression none the less steady.

The hollow mask of friendship, of reciprocal
sympathy and confidence was still kept up between
him and Countess Szent Imre; indeed, on either side
no opportunity was lost, as if in self-defence—or,
at any rate, in self-delusion—of laying the utmost
stress on the purely friendly nature of their relations.

An incident occurred about that time, trifling, no
doubt, in itself, but nevertheless sufficient to serve
as a warning to George, had he been in the frame
of mind to listen to it.

One of Countess Szent Imre's favourite cobs had

gone lame; so she suggested trying Lord George's pony in double harness, with the intention of buying it, should it be found to match. The latter of course, assented to this, fervently hoping that old Fobs would be found to pull too hard for the Countess's delicate hands, or otherwise not to suit her: for he saw no chance of replacing him within three or four weeks' time. The pony, a nice-looking brown with smartish action, behaved to perfection on his first trial in double harness, when the Countess and his master took the phaeton out for a turn around the park.

It was a lovely spring morning; a south-westerly breeze had melted away the last remnants of snow that a few days ago still lay in small patches under the hedges, where the snowdrops were timidly surging from the frost-bound soil. The sun was shining brightly, and in the distance the first notes of the cuckoo were faintly heard.

"Upon my word," said the Countess, after having driven in silence for some minutes, "do you know I think he will do; but I must drive them myself by-and-by. They certainly go very nicely with you, though they have not got quite the same action."

"No, they haven't," answered George. "Besides, I don't really know that I can let you have old Fobs at once. You see, I should have nothing left to get about with myself."

The Countess is far too good a judge of "pace" —metaphorically speaking—to have any misgivings as to his consenting eventually. After a few seconds of silence, she turns her eyes upon him and says, in rather a softer tone:

"Not if *I* asked you?"

The question was one not very easily answered, when sitting so close to an exceedingly fascinating woman that her arm was touching his, and when two wondrous green eyes were turned upon him with a look of earnest appeal which she could give them at any moment, whether in earnest or in jest.

Now of course, prudence and wisdom would have suggested to this misguided young man a vaguely evasive answer, a rapid return of thought to his old love far away, possibly a speedy retreat from a vicinity the dangers of which were becoming rather more marked, under the plea of a sudden headache caused by the balmy spring air.

George Mansfield did nothing of all this; but, turning his head towards her, he said, half jestingly:

"What will you give me if I let you have the pony at once—I don't mean what *price?*"

"Unconditional surrender are my terms," said Countess Szent Imre. "But we must have that hood up; it is coming on to rain; what a bore it is!"

A few clouds had rapidly been gathering, and a smart shower—no unusual occurrence at the time of year—was coming down. The hood is put up, and for a few minutes they drive along in silence, the feeling of close proximity to each other and seclusion from the rest of the world being somewhat intensified by the covering which shuts off the view on either side.

At last George Mansfield breaks the silence:

"What would you give to have at this moment the *right man* sitting here in my place?"

The Countess is by no means taken aback, and answers most imperturbably: "How do you know there is a right man?"

"Well, if there is not, men in your country must be very different from what they are in ours," says George sententiously; and he gently touches up his pony, who is beginning slightly to flag.

"And supposing there were"—and, like a flash of lightning, those green eyes are seen to sparkle— "what do you imagine he would say?"

"I don't know what he would say—I know what he would do," George answers, in a short, rather abrupt tone, as if struggling with himself.

At this moment their conversation is interrupted by a gate which the groom has to descend to open. Sitting behind the hood, he, of course, saw none of the by-play of a conversation carried on in a language unintelligible to him.

The thread was broken, and the few remarks exchanged before the castle was once more reached, referred to the pony, who, the Countess finally decided, was not a sufficiently good match for hers.

"I suppose I shall see you again before long?" were her parting words, and her hand just dwelt the tenth part of a second in his.

Spring gradually waned into summer, and the monotony of the riding-school was varied by frequent days of squadron drill. On returning one morning

with his troop, after three hours hard work, George
was rather surprised to find an order from his Colonel to report himself at headquarters the following
morning.   He had by that time been some eight or
nine months with the regiment, and felt thoroughly
at home in all his varied duties.   So it was with a
feeling more of curiosity than of apprehension that
he set off to obey the summons.

Having given the orders for the day to his senior
sergeant-major, he mounted his second charger,
rather looking forward to his ride, which was nearly
all over grass, and to a day with his brother officers.
Cantering along over the fine springy turf, the wiry
chestnut he was riding just catching hold nicely,
George could not but say to himself that, after all,
things had not turned out as badly as they might.
His work was thoroughly congenial to him; he had
found nothing but friendship and kindness in his
new sphere of life; and some day things might right
themselves.

Anyhow, he felt he had done his duty towards
Mildred in begging her not to allow any consideration for himself to affect her plans for the future.
Of course he loved her still just the same, and would
never care for any other woman; no, not in the same
way, at least!   At this phase of his meditations the
image of the lovely Countess came back to his mind
and, together with it, every word of their conversation in the park.   Had he anything to reproach himself with?   No, surely not; it had all been harmless
chaff.   Besides, her thoughts were evidently ab-

sorbed by another than himself; so why should he, from any sort of groundless scruples, deprive himself of the charm of her society, which had slowly grown into a very important feature in his solitary existence?

Nevertheless, his range of thoughts as he gradually approached the outskirts of Toronya did not, from the expression of his countenance, appear to be an altogether unpleasant one; and any pity which his friends at home might have bestowed upon him for living in some outlandish place would have been altogether wasted just then.

His Colonel's greeting was most friendly. He told George the matter he wished to talk over with him was a private one, and thereupon requested him to sit down. He then began thus:

"I wish you to understand that all I am going to say is said exclusively in your own interest. I have had a very good account of you throughout, and what I have seen of your troop shows me that you have worked hard and entirely understand your duties. So far, so good; I must now pass on to a matter to which I shall refer—please mark this—more as a friend than as your commanding officer. Of course we all know that when you joined you were heavily in debt. No formal understanding was entered upon, fixing any particular date at which these liabilities were to be settled; but from the correspondence that passed on the subject I gather, firstly, that every effort would be made to settle the matter within a reasonable time; secondly, that it was not expected that any of your creditors would, what I may call, become troublesome. I need hardly add that, were it otherwise, your chance of being accepted in our army would indeed have been a poor one.

"As to the first point; I am not aware how much nearer its accomplishment you are now than when you first joined. With regard to the second, a somewhat unpleasant incident has occurred. Having previously applied unsuccessfully to Lord Errington, a London firm, signing themselves "Messrs. Smith & Walter, Turf Accountants," have written to the War Office in Vienna, inquiring as to your whereabouts, and your ability to settle. I have no doubt you have found out by now how exceedingly particular we are about this sort of thing. Many a young fellow has lost his commission for far smaller sums than what I understand you to owe. It has been thus with us for generations back, and we know of no exception.

"The letter has been transmitted to me by the War Office; they are a good deal annoyed, and it would not do if it were to happen again. You had better answer the letter yourself; but, at the same time, I am instructed to impress upon you the extreme desirability of getting your affairs settled between this and, say six months' time. Nothing has actually been said in so many words as to the consequences any further delay might have; but I am bound to tell you I am afraid they might be serious. I have a high opinion of you as an officer, and I

think you may have a distinguished future before
you; therefore I am acting only as a friend in putting this before you plainly. I have nothing more
to add."

George had but little to say in reply, beyond
expressing his willingness to do all that lay in his
power; and he withdrew shortly afterwards. He
felt greatly perturbed by what he had just heard.
He fully understood the ominous hints the Colonel
had thrown out; but, on the other hand, expecting
him to square his position within six months, was
obviously expecting him to do what was beyond his
power. With his spirits at rather a low ebb, he
made his day at headquarters shorter than he had
originally intended, and the falling night found him
back again in his country retreat.

CHAPTER XI.

"Go not, happy day,
    From the shining fields,
Go not, happy day,
    Till the maiden yields.

"Rosy is the West,
    Rosy is the South,
Roses are her cheeks,
    And a rose her mouth.

"When the happy Yes
    Falters from her lips,
Pass and blush the news
    Over glowing ships."
                                TENNYSON.

MILDRED CHARTERIS, on returning to her quiet
country home in Hampshire after her visit to Mrs.
Jack Arthur, once more calmly and cheerfully took
up the thread of her peaceful and somewhat monotonous existence. Time never seemed to hang
on her hands, perhaps owing to the fact of her devoting so little of it to herself. In her quiet, un-
ostentatious way she would visit the cottages of all
to whom she thought her presence might offer relief, and at many a bedside was her pure, placid
countenance lighted upon by eyes destined shortly
to be closed.

The letter which she had received from George
Mansfield, urging her once more to let herself be
hampered by no consideration for him, had come
rather as a shock to her feelings, but she endeavoured to persuade herself that this was nothing
but the outcome of a generous wish of repairing any
wrong he might have committed towards her. Hers
was one of those natures leaving unto Providence the
care for the morrow, and the making of plans found
no room in her day's work.

Soon after they had parted she had written Lord
Devereux a short letter, only repeating in other words
what she had already told him at Manor Lodge,
and asking him to forgive her if her answer had
wounded his feelings. His reply was couched in
such generous and noble-minded words that, slow of
belief though she was on that subject, she could not
but realise the full depth of his affection for her.

She was strolling about her garden one morning,
attending to the wants of her favourite flowers, when
a letter, addressed in George Mansfield's familiar
hand, was brought her. These had gradually become somewhat less frequent of late, for George
would plead the absence of any material whatever
from which to concoct a letter—a sure sign, were
others wanting, of love on the wane: for was ever a
lover known who could not, at any given moment,
cover twelve pages without conveying a single par-
ticle of news?

Without avoiding to mention Countess Szent
Imre's name when writing to Mildred, George's re-

ferences to her had of late grown scarce; and likewise in this particular letter he said no more than
that he had been dining with her once or twice during
the preceding week. The interview with his Colonel,
however, he related most fully, drawing the most
gloomy forebodings from it. He wound up by saying:

"It is all very well their talking, but you know
how absurd the idea is of my being able to raise six
or seven thousand pounds between this and the end
of the year; allowing for the small amounts I have
been steadily paying off, it will take quite that to
set me right. It is impossible.

"I am afraid they really mean I cannot remain
in the army unless the matter is settled, and if I
have to throw up the sponge, Heaven only knows
what is to become of me. Here I am doing well,
and have some chance of getting on. I like my
work, and have got used by now to the life. I am
beginning to fear all my efforts will be wasted; perhaps before very long you will see me driving an
omnibus down Piccadilly. It does seem awfully
hard, but I don't blame them; I mean the military
authorities here. They are quite as much down
upon their own fellows, and, of course, it would not
do to make exceptions for a foreigner.

"I am sorry to give you such a gloomy account. I was beginning to get quite hopeful a little
time ago, but now everything looks worse than ever."

Mildred felt deeply depressed by the receipt of
this letter. The idea of George's returning home

again after a year of his life wasted, and utterly
disheartened at his abortive attempt at righting himself, haunted her during many a sleepless night; but,
turn it over in her mind as she would, not a ray of
light would appear to guide her in the utter darkness that had befallen her. And yet she knew that
from her alone could advice or assistance come. She
was well aware that no power on earth could induce
George to apply to his brother even for a temporary
loan, and that he would merely await his fate in
passive resignation.

A heavy cloud of anxiety and suspense thus
hung over the young girl's life; the look of placid
serenity upon her countenance had given way to
an expression of intense mental strain. She was
in the midst of one of these fits of sombre meditation when a telegram was handed her. It ran thus:

"Am staying at the Willows until Monday; will
call to-morrow tea-time.

"DEVEREUX."

She had not seen the sender of this message
since they stayed together under Mrs. Jack Arhur's
roof, and though her first impression was rather to
dread an interview which could not fail to bring
back painful recollections, she at the same time
felt gratified by this additional proof on Lord Devereux's part that no resentment was rankling in his
mind.

Her manner was perfectly natural on greeting

him the following day and her welcome most cordial.
Before they had been together many minutes, Lord
Devereux had noticed the weary, wan look upon the
pale face on which his eyes were resting.

"Miss Charteris," he began, "you told me you
wished to keep me as a friend though I could be
nothing more. You are not given to making
speeches you do not mean, so I will avail myself at
once of the privilege you have granted me. You
are not looking yourself, and your bright, cheery
manner has gone. What is it? Ill-health; or have
you had any troubles or worries that I do not know
of? And, if the latter, may I claim the privilege of
your confiding in me? You must not look on me
as a fine weather friend; you will find enough of
these and to spare. Keep me for troubled times;
entrust me with all that weighs upon your mind.
Perhaps I can guess the quarter from which the
trouble comes; but do not let the wish of avoiding
me any unnecessary pain stop you; I am pretty well
hardened against pain since these last few months."

Tears have gathered in Mildred's lustrous eyes
whilst Lord Devereux was speaking, and she answers:

"Yes, I will look upon you as a friend. I am a
bad hand at little conventional falsehoods, so I will
tell you the whole truth. I have a heavy sorrow
weighing upon my mind. You have guessed rightly,
I have no doubt, where it comes from. Poor dear!
it is no fault of his; he has been behaving admirably
and has slaved away night and day, but they now
tell him that unless his debts are paid by the end

of the year he will have to leave the Austrian service. If he does it will make him perfectly reckless, and there is no saying what the end will be. Forgive me if I am hurting your feelings—I never do anything else: Heaven knows I would not do so willingly, but you asked me to tell you the truth."

Lord Devereux never winced, and when Mildred had ceased speaking he said, in a tone altogether devoid of the earnestness of his former words:

"I cannot tell you how sorry I am. Poor fellow! I fancy he lost most of it over that little mare of mine, did not he? She has won a lot of races since. I suppose Errington's agent, old Milton, looks after George's affairs too, doesn't he?" And thereupon he changed the subject, doing his best to cheer Mildred's spirits by rattling along in his old-fashioned, anecdotic manner.

Shortly afterwards he took his departure, and Mildred could not help noticing his springy, elastic gait as he went to meet his horse that was just being brought round, and the cheery ring of his voice as he bade her farewell.

Three days later Mildred received the following letter:

DEAR MISS CHARTERIS,—I devoutly hope you may never have any worse troubles in life than those you told me about the other day, and if this letter can bring back the smiles to your lips I shall bless Mrs. Ramsay for having asked me down to The Willows last week.

Anyhow, it is all right. I saw old Milton two days after I left you. Things are not half as bad as I had expected. In any case, the receipts will be in Milton's hands within very few days.

I have instructed him not to mention my name and not to write to our friend for the present, as he had better leave that to your tact.

Don't trouble to answer this, and believe me,

Yours ever,

DEVEREUX.

Mildred's first sensation on receiving this letter was a rush of deep and overwhelming gratitude for so unexpected and spontaneous an act of generosity on the part of Lord Devereux towards the very man who, as he well knew, had from the first stood in the way of the accomplishment of all his heart's desires. The extreme simplicity and want of ostentation with which it was done impressed her more almost than the act itself, and never before or after was Lord Devereux so near to her heart as at that moment.

On the other hand, when cooler reflection set in, she could not but realise that this act placed her under a deep and lifelong obligation towards him, as the chance of the sum being repaid was obviously a remote one. Though she knew Lord Devereux too well to think for a moment that he would ever attempt to take advantage of this position, her sense of justice, together with her quickness of perception, soon revealed to her the dilemma she was placed in.

In her sad perplexity she bethought herself of her friend, Mrs. Garrard, from whom she had received a letter that very morning, saying she was going up to town for three or four days.

"I know I can trust her," she said to herself, "and she knows so much more of the world than I do." The two had corresponded frequently during the last few months, besides having met at a County Ball in the course of the spring, and they now looked at each other quite in the light of old friends.

Before the next hour was over, a message was flashing up to London: "Want you badly; do come down to dine and sleep. If impossible, will be in town to-morrow."

Mrs. Garrard, warm-hearted and impulsive, like most of her countrywomen, guessed there must be some serious reason for Mildred to send for her in this manner; so, leaving her own affairs to take care of themselves, she dashed off to Waterloo, and, by five o'clock, the two friends were drinking tea together. Their greeting was a genuinely affectionate one, with that true ring which no amount of tawdry gush can replace.

Mrs. Garrard had far too much tact to begin with cross-questioning Mildred as to "what was the matter?" but she was not kept long in suspense. When the tale was told, her delicate features assumed an expression of deep reflection.

"My dear child," she said, "this is indeed a hard case, if ever there was one. It would not be so to many people, for lots of girls would simply jump at

the idea of becoming Lady Devereux, whilst others
would accept his money for their young friend, would
say 'Thank you!' and then cry quits. Of course, I
know you are different or you would not have required my advice. People will say unkind things—
at least the mothers of girls who have been knocking
about London ball-rooms for five or six seasons will.
You don't mind that, do you?"

Mildred shakes her head.

"Do you think for a moment Lord Devereux
looks upon it at all in the light of a bargain? Excuse
my cross-questioning you—but I *must!*"

"No, I am positive he does not."

"Do you actually dislike him—I mean, does he
grate on your nerves? Do you hate the sight of him
when he says all the pretty things I have no doubt
he has said?"

"My dear Maggie," the young girl says, colouring
slightly, "what questions you do ask! No, I can't
say I dislike him at all—least of all now, when he
has behaved so nobly. But surely that is not enough
reason to wish to marry him, is it?"

"Dear child! I married for love, and the result
has not been a very satisfactory one, has it? But I
really cannot solve these problems upon which the
happiness of half-a-dozen people may depend, at five
minutes' notice. I will think it over between this
and dinner-time, and before you go to bed to-night
you shall have my opinion on the matter. Will that
do; and shall I sing you something now?"

The soft notes of her pure, melodious voice had

a soothing effect upon the poor girl's distracted
nerves, and, in the pleasure of her friend's company, she forgot for the moment her harassing per-
plexities.

They had one more talk in Mildred's bedroom
before she put out her candles.

"Mildred," Mrs. Garrard said in a quiet but
rather decided tone, "I have thought it over and I
think you ought to marry Lord Devereux. After all,
when all our ingenuity fails, don't you think the old
test of right and wrong is the simplest and safest
one. Lord Devereux knows you are not in love
with him and knows how much he can expect. To
take his money (for practically the money is given
to you) in the hopes of its setting George Mansfield
right and your eventually marrying him, would be
mean and unworthy of you; and as to your letting
George go to the wall when it is in your power to
save him—I know you won't do that. Now, don't
look too tragic over it, child, for there really is no
occasion to do so. I know exactly what you feel
like; shall I tell you? I dare say you have never
been to Tattersall's: 'And only six thousand bid for
her, no more; six thousand; have you all done; going
at six thousand; gone!'" and she brings her hand
down on the table, endeavouring with her rings to
imitate the rattle of the hammer. "Don't think me
unsympathising, for you know I am not. Now go to
sleep and try not to think any more about it."

Mildred could not resist bursting out laughing
at the latter part of Mrs. Garrard's peroration, for it

reflected, with too painful accuracy, the exact state of her feelings. After her friend had left, she spent half-an-hour in silent prayer, and when she rose, her mind was made up. She had decided to sacrifice herself for George's sake.

What is called in French a "combat de générosité," though a frequent occurrence on the stage, is somewhat rare in real life. Anyhow, Lord Devereux, who was a warm-hearted English gentleman, and not a fanatic of the flagellant type, allowed his scruples of delicacy to be overruled without any very great difficulty, and within a week the engagement was announced, *urbi et orbi.*

Mildred's task of informing George of the turn things had taken was by no means an easy one, owing to her extreme anxiety to prevent his noticing any direct connection between the two items of news she was imparting to him. Sooner than wound his delicacy, she took upon herself the stigma of having, of her own free will, finally relented towards Lord Devereux's reiterated proposals.

With regard to the financial difficulty, which George had been complaining about to her, she contrived, with consummate tact, to put the matter before him in the light of a loan Lord Devereux was making him to enable him to stay in his profession, and chiefly on account of a large part of his losses having arisen from having followed Lord Devereux's advice about backing his stable.

CHAPTER XII.

"Let the sweet heavens endure,
    Not close and darken above me,
Before I am quite, quite sure
    That there is one to love me;
Then let come what come may
    To a life that has been so sad,
    I shall have had my day."

TENNYSON.

At what stage in the proceedings and by what symptoms does a man find out that he is "in love;" and more especially so when there is no one to "make the running" for him, and when whatever competition may exist does not meet his eye in the tangible shape of a rival, but is known to him only from the accounts given by the lady of his affection, which will in many, if not most, cases be slightly touched up with a view either of increasing or minimising their importance—as may suit her purpose?

No one will gainsay that circumstances were singularly propitious towards George Mansfield's sooner or later falling a victim to the charms of the lovely Hungarian Countess. Like the germ of any epidemic that thrives and takes root under certain conditions only, and will not be absorbed by the system under certain others, likewise the germ of

love may fall on barren soil and may die away,
when, under different circumstances in the same individual, it might have spread and grown and
developed itself.

Thus a life full of varied interests, distractions
and excitements might have proved a safeguard to
poor George Mansfield, whereas the many solitary
evenings, with no companions but his books, left
him time for fits of brooding, for going over in his
mind the words he had heard the evening before,
and for working himself into a thoroughly dangerous
frame of mind. Nothing was more characteristic of
the change he had undergone unwittingly than the
manner in which he received Mildred's communication. The pang he felt at first at the announcement
of her engagement—vaguely anticipated though it
might have been—was very severe; but it was un-
questionably much relieved by the knowledge that he
would not be again cast adrift, and could persevere
in the path he had cut out for himself.

As to Lord Devereux's timely assistance, the
amount of which would, of course, eventually be re-
funded in full, he persuaded himself to look upon it as
a generous, but, considering all the circumstances, by
no means unaccountable act. Anyhow, Mildred was
now lost to him—irretrievably lost. She would soon
be another's. His face hardened at the thought;
what could it matter now to anyone what he did,
he asked himself, in a fit of utter recklessness, as
he rode off to impart the news to the fair hostess of
Kisfalva.

The tone in which she expressed her deep sympathy for him had such a genuine ring, and was expressed so unreservedly, that George began to feel that this was hardly quite the effect he had hoped his communication to produce.

Countess Szent Imre was reclining on a chaise-longue in the boudoir in which she had, for the first time, received George. The windows were thrown wide open to let in the balmy spring air; a few steps led from the room down to the terrace, resplendent with many-coloured flower-beds, that did much credit to the English head-gardener, whom Count Szent Imre had persuaded to bring about a metamorphosis in the long-neglected gardens of his ancestral mansion. Beyond the garden the eye could rest on the vast expanse of the park; and, still farther, the snow-clad range of the Carpathian Mountains appeared against the horizon.

"Come and take a walk in the garden," said Countess Szent Imre: "it is wicked sitting indoors on a day like this; and don't look depressed if you can help it, for I am rather down on my luck my-self to-day. I suppose you are awfully cut up—are you? I am so sorry. As long as you do not ask me to comfort you —at least, not to-day! for I am much too busy moaning over my own fate. No: but seriously" (raising her eyes from the ground, and letting them shine for the first time during their conversation upon him in their full radiancy) "I am awfully sorry for you. I suppose you are jealous, too—are you?" This last question was asked in a tone of half-wondering curiosity, such as might be adopted in inquiring from a patient as to some new and strange symptom of his malady. "Poor boy! I wonder what it feels like! Somehow, it seems so long since I felt anything of the kind. I suppose you won't go over for the wedding, will you?"

George's acquaintance with the Countess was long and intimate enough by that time for him to know that, in certain of her moods, it was quite useless to endeavour to divert her thoughts into any channel other than the one she would let them drift into. He quickly noticed that on that day they were wandering far away, and that any attempt of his to try and improve the shining hour would prove wholly futile. Thus conversation lingered on. Never had Countess Szent Imre, in George's eyes, appeared more absolutely bewitching. Her slim, graceful figure was clearly defined in the white serge suit she was wearing—the sailor's hat, resting on the thick curls of auburn hair, and its gay ribbon, seemed thoroughly in keeping with the look of almost child-like playfulness which her countenance would now and then take.

"Don't go yet," she said to George, who was making preparations for his departure. "I know you have found me very dull to-day. Don't be angry; I could not help it. My thoughts had been wandering in the past when you came, and, somehow, your story made me worse."

The clouds were gathering on her brow unnoticed by George; for she spoke as if to herself, with her head almost turned away from him. After a moment's silence, she addressed him again in her low, musical voice.

"I had always meant to tell you some day what I am now going to say. It is better for you that you should hear it; there is but one other person in the world who knows of it. But I think I can trust you. Well! what I am going to tell you is practically the history of my life. Don't be alarmed; I am not very old, and my story is not very long—in fact, I dare say, a very commonplace one. Of course, you know I was left a widow when little more than a child. It was then that I met the man whom I cared for, not wisely, but too well. I was everything to him—my youth, my hopes, my faith in mankind were laid down at his feet. The object of my life was to please him, and to make him happy; and two years of my life passed like a dream. One morning I received an anonymous letter telling me the man in whom I placed a world of faith, for whose sake I would have committed every crime, passed his leisure hours with a circus rider. She was a very smart girl—I can see her now; she used to ride the *haute école* on a little weedy thoroughbred. You can guess the rest. Don't think I am like the woman in the tragedy, who stamps up and down the stage, vowing vengeance on the whole sex because one man has deceived her; not at all! Do you ever read Schiller?

'Ich habe genossen das irdische Glück,
Ich habe gelebt und geliebet.'

"I was once full of girlish innocence and candour

and faith; that was what God made me: what you
see now is man's work. I have only very little more
to add. Your life is empty in a great many ways;
you have had a great blow in your dearest affections,
two reasons for which you might before very long
work up your imagination into fancying yourself in
love with me. Mark my words; don't! I don't go
in for little flirtations, as I have told you before. I
like you very well as a friend; there are moments
when I fancy I might drift into caring for you in a
sort of way. It would be the greatest misfortune for
you, for I know I could make you love me, and I
have nothing really to give in return. My life lies
in the past and the requiescat on that grave can
never be moved. And now you had better go. You
are sure you won't stay and dine?"

Slowly did George Mansfield wend his way home
that evening; the rich springy turf he had to ride
over could not tempt him to go out of a foot's-pace,
with the reins hanging loosely on his horse's neck.
Needless to say, he lighted a cigar—in the frame of
mind he was in, every man does—regardless of the
delicious fragrance of the violets that lined his path.

He felt that afternoon would be a landmark in
his life. The tale he had just heard, told, with the
utmost simplicity, in short, almost abrupt sentences,
had stirred him to the very innermost depths of
his soul.

On returning to his own fireside he was not
altogether pleasantly surprised to find Father Vincent
waiting for him. Though this was not in itself an

infrequent occurrence, he felt that on this particular evening he could well have dispensed with any other company than that of his own meditations. Nevertheless he had too much regard for the priest's extremely sensitive feelings not to give him a cheery welcome and to invite him to share his frugal supper.

Father Vincent appeared to be in a more communicative mood and altogether in better spirits than was his wont; so much so that George could not refrain from noticing it to him.

"You are quite right," said the latter; "I feel quite cheerful to-day. A priest's life is a hard one, especially if he does not live merely for the routine work, but tries to do some permanent good. After years of opposition I have at last had the necessary funds assured me for building and maintaining a little cottage-hospital for our village: not more than six beds to begin with, but anyhow it will be an improvement upon the present state of things. Yes, I feel as elated as you would after—well, I suppose after winning a race or securing the affections of some lovely girl whom you hoped to make your wife?"

"But, Father Vincent," was George's answer, "does *all* your happiness in life consist in doing good to others? Do you never think of yourself? Of course, I fully realise that from most forms of self-indulgence you are debarred; but for all that, there must be many pleasures, wholly innocent, which might be within your reach. Have they no attraction for you?"

"None whatever," was the priest's reply. "I entered holy orders as a Franciscan monk. The founder of our order had enjoyed life's merriment for a short while, indeed—and he turned from it in weariness and disgust. He was a saint long before he was canonised, and we try to learn from his experience. He wished us to live as the birds of the air do, trusting to Providence alone for our maintenance. To us the word pleasure has no other meaning than helping our fellow-creatures. My father was a well-to-do man down in the south of Hungary. He wanted me to enter the Bar, and I had completed all my studies. Now I would not change with the Prime Minister, let alone with a barrister. What does ambition mean? Can it matter to anybody whether he is forgotten ten years after his death, as the Prime Minister will be; or twenty-four hours after it, as I shall? Is it not exactly the same when you think of eternity? And you who, as you have often told me yourself, have lived for pleasure alone, has your life been a happy one altogether? Are you sure of obtaining all your heart longs for? Are you sure, if you do obtain it, the fruit may not die away in your hand the moment it is picked, and leave you nothing but remorse and disillusion? And then you will begin afresh, pursuing some new purpose, and so on. Is that happiness?"

Had George been similarly addressed a year or two previously, the chances are that he would have declined the discussion of so abstruse a subject with the remark that the views of a soldier and of a

monk were scarcely likely to coincide on such a
topic, possibly accompanied by a cheque for the
benefit of the hospital in which his companion was
interested. But, under the circumstances, although
it appeared to him that the conversation was getting
rather too much within the range of personalities, he
answered without any endeavour to change the topic.

"Of course, happiness and pleasure are, to my
mind at least, two totally different things. To make
the search of pleasure one's sole object in life is, no
doubt, characteristic of a shallow and almost contemptible nature; but to aim at happiness for oneself, and not only for others, as you do, appears to
me a perfectly legitimate purpose. What it consists
in will probably never be defined, and I suppose
everybody is the best judge in his own case. You
will not eradicate that pursuit of happiness from
human nature, any more than you will the instinct
of self-preservation, by any amount of preaching. I
don't mean you, personally, of course; it is irrespec-
tive of age, and nationality, and creed. A very small
percentage of philanthropists—so small that they almost disappear amongst the number, has probably
existed at all times. I take it they are *born* as such.
I do not want for a moment to dispute the utter
unselfishness of their motives; but if they take
pleasure in doing acts of charity, it is no longer any
sacrifice to them, and consequently, as far as they
themselves are concerned, there can be no merit left,
if the merit of an action is to be judged, not by the
results—which would be manifestly unfair—but by

the amount of self-denial to which it gave rise. I do
not wish to appear cynical or materialistic. If I were
to give up everything in life—that would not mean
very much just now—and were to turn monk, it
would be, indeed, an act of self-sacrifice. But in
your case—I hope I am not shocking your feelings
—you are born for self-abnegation, and would have
practised it before the founder of your Order ever
lived—before the Christian era began."

"You are not wounding my feelings in any way,"
the priest answered mildly; "but you cannot expect
me to agree with your views. It is a matter that
admits of no absolutely conclusive demonstration;
but my experience of humanity leads me to doubt
in the love of the fellow-creature existing, so to speak,
as a *taste*, as you might care for books or for racing.
I have no faith in your *born* philanthropist; and, believe me, were it not for the deepest and most
earnest religious feeling, few would take to the life
we lead. The love of our fellow-creatures is merely
the offspring of religion. I love the poor and the
suffering *now*; I thought but little about them before I entered holy orders. Do you believe in the
efficacy of charity when unaccompanied by the true
humility of heart that lowers you to the level of the
poor you are visiting, or rather raises them to yours?
I know you look upon me rather in the light of some
strange animal, what I should call a 'lusus naturæ,'
though many of my brethren have practised self-
abnegation far more than I have. Happiness without
faith is a thing I cannot imagine the existence of.

Don't you think yourself that weary, restless look I
see so often upon your countenance would vanish if
you could bring yourself to look beyond the narrow
boundaries of this present life, and not to endeavour
to cram so much enjoyment and excitement into the
short span of time that is allotted you? Forgive the
warmth with which I speak. Do not put it down to
any professional zeal or any narrow-minded proselytism. I know that religion in most modern
societies is reduced to a purely conventional form,
and that strength of mind and strength of will are
required to rouse oneself from following the beaten
track and doing as others do. That would be the
first step towards real happiness. Practise renunciation and self-sacrifice; it will give you before long a
far keener enjoyment than any you have tasted as
yet. Like the alchemists of old, who wasted years of
their life in the futile endeavour of making gold,
placing first one substance and then another into the
cauldron, hoping first exultingly, then wearily that
the deposit left by the combination of all these different ores blended together might be the coveted
yellow metal; likewise he who lives only for the
vanities of this world throws everything that can at-
tract and allure the senses into the cauldron, from
which he hopes to distil happiness. He piles them
one on the other—every pleasure, enjoyment and
delectation; his life is replete with them. But, like
the alchemist, he waits in vain."

George had but little to say in reply to the ex-
ordium addressed to him with an amount of warmth

and depth of feeling which lighted up the priest's
countenance with a look of the noblest fervour that
ever shone upon the face of any martyr, fearlessly
awaiting his doom in the Amphitheatre of Flavius.
Had he replied his words would probably have been,
that theoretically he could but agree with all the
priest's views, but that he could find no application
to them as far as his own life was concerned; and
yet the virtue of self-abnegation need not be shunned
from want of opportunity of exercising it.

George's slumbers were restless that night.
Scenes followed each other without intermission before his mind, like glimpses of Holbein's "Devils'
Dance," seen through a magic lantern. First he saw
Mildred in bridal attire and with the orange blossoms
in her hair, standing before the altar, pale as are the
dead. He felt her turn her eyes upon him in earnest
entreaty. Then, suddenly, she held out her arms
towards him—not lovingly, but beseechingly, as if
calling upon him to save her. But some superior
power rooted him to the ground and held him
motionless.

The scene vanished; and soon he saw before
him the features, pale and ascetic, of the friar, holding up to him the cross, the emblem of his order;
and as he talked to him the figure of the monk
seemed to multiply as if his brethren had risen and
were joining him, and were encircling the spot where
George stood, and he felt himself carried away, as if
ready and willing to follow them, until his eye caught
sight of the Countess, temptingly bewitching, watch-

ing the scene from a balcony above. The noble
features he loved to gaze upon were lighted up by
a smile—placid, indifferent, perhaps almost con-
temptuous. No glance of encouragement met his
eye; but none was required. He fought his way
through the crowd surging densely around him
towards where the lovely form stood, and, looking
up, he saw the set expression had melted to one of
passionate wistfulness and softness, and from under
the drooping lids shot forth one glance like a
Parthian arrow—as straight, almost as deadly.

George was rudely awakened and brought back
to stern reality by a knock at his door, and the appearance of his sergeant-major making his daily
report. One man laid up with fever, and a charger
lame from having caught his leg in the collar rein.

"Of course, the best one out of the lot must go
and lame himself," said George rather moodily; "why
can't the fool of a man see to the weights working
properly; a horse cannot get caught if they do. The
men to turn out in full marching order at my door
at three this afternoon. Troop to parade at seven
this morning for squadron drill; remounts to be left
at home."

About an hour later George could be seen riding
off at the head of his troop, in the direction of the
large plain where three squadrons were under orders
to meet.

CHAPTER XIII.

"We met in secret in the depth of night,
  When there was none to watch us; not an eye,
  Save the lone dweller of the lonely sky,
To gaze upon our love and pure delight:
And in that hour's unbroken solitude,
  When the white moon had robed her in its beams,
  I thought some vision of a blessed dream
Or spirit of the air before me stood
And held communion with me."

ISMAEL FITZADAM.

IT was not often that Countess Szent Imre indulged in a retrospect of her past life towards
others; and long after George had left she remained
musing, as if exhausted by the effort of lifting the
veil from off the history of her life.

What she had told George was the truth. She
had loved once only, but then with all the passion
of a Southern nature. There was nothing petty
about her; and when she felt she had met what was
to be the love of her life, she gave herself away,
body and soul, to the man she loved, as Cleopatra
might have done to Antony, in true queenly fashion,
with none of the little artifices and subterfuges and
sham resistances characteristic of the *fin de siècle*
romance.

The man through whom the whole current of

her life was to be altered had first attracted her attention by a speech he had made in the Hungarian House of Lords during a debate at which she happened to be present. The discussion was a stormy one, as is frequently the case in that Parliament, which, despite its venerable age, has still maintained a more than youthful vigour, and in which but a light spark is required to bring about a conflagration.

Count Kesthelyi, who to an unusually fascinating appearance added many of the charms of manner so frequently found in the Hungarian magnate, rose when the excitement was at its culminating point. He then occupied a position analogous to what an Under-Secretary of State is with us.

A violent attack had been directed against the department which he was called upon to represent on account of an apparent breach of duty committed by one of the minor officials. Strong words, such as "corruption" and "venality," had been freely bandied about, when amidst breathless silence, the Under-Secretary rose to his feet. In a few short sentences, pronounced in a tone of the most perfectly imperturbable urbanity, he destroyed the hollow fabric of empty words that had been directed against him. It would have been easy to extricate himself and the cabinet from the awkward position they were placed in, by sacrificing the subordinate official against whom the brunt of the attack was directed. Too proud to do this he declared himself fully responsible for the other's actions. Did anybody suspect *him* of venality, let him say so outside the

10*

walls of the House, when an answer would be speedily forthcoming.

There are perhaps few nations in which the ring of chivalrous words and actions will so freely find an echo as in the Hungarian. The Government obtained an overwhelming majority, and Count Kesthelyi was the hero of the day. Chance would have it that the following day Countess Szent Imre met him at dinner. They had been nothing but the most ordinary acquaintances until then; but a few hours are often sufficient to decide upon the destiny of a life.

Far from being elated, or apparently even conscious of the success he had achieved the man whose name was now in everybody's mouth appeared rather disposed to avoid the topic of last night's debate—an unusual thing in a man barely out of his twenties —and to turn the conversation rather upon her than upon himself. They soon began to see more of each other; she, the widow of twenty-one, with all the sweet fragrance of youth upon her; he, fascinating, clever and agreeable, but unfettered by any principles as far as the fair sex was concerned. Like many of his compatriots, he had been, when hardly more than a boy, forced rather reluctantly into a marriage which family considerations made desirable: an ill-fated union which, after very few years, remained a union but in name.

Anything savouring of deceit and treachery was altogether foreign to Countess Szent Imre's nature, such as it was at that time. A childless widow, she

felt as if she had no one to consult but the voice of
her own heart, and she followed it. Radiantly happy
as she was during the few years that followed, unknown to herself a slow process of moral dissolution
was at work within her—the unavoidable consequence
of a life destined at least to deceive the world at
large; and nothing was done on the part of her
brilliant but singularly unscrupulous lover to arrest
the progress of it. Illusions followed the way scruples
had gone, and the ennobling influence of a wholly
unselfish passion alone kept up some of the better
qualities of a nature gifted far above the average of
her sex. When the man to whom she had given
everything finally deceived her with a low circus-
rider, she went through as dangerous a crisis as ever
was woman's fate to survive. Though vaguely suspected by some, the fiery tumult that raged within
her breast for many months was never allowed to
become public property; and shortly afterwards she
married Count Szent Imre, her senior by many years,
who expected little more from his wife than that her
lovely presence should grace his board and should
do the honours of his house in the manner that had
become a tradition of it.

This was the woman that stern Fate threw across
poor George Mansfield's path. Love such as hers
does not become extinct this side of the grave.
"What is pride, compared with love?" she would
say wistfully to herself; and had Count Kesthelyi
come back penitent, no doubt his misdeeds would
have found forgiveness in her eyes. But there was

not the faintest indication of his having any such intention.

A sudden return to the frankness and straightforwardness of olden days had impelled her to give George Mansfield, for whom she felt a considerable amount of sympathy, the warning chronicled before.

Three or four weeks have elapsed. Wild work has been wrought in George Mansfield's feverish mind. Had Countess Szent Imre been bent upon fanning the flame of passion within him she could not have done so more effectively than by the words she had spoken. His mind was becoming more and more absorbed by her; and though he went through all his professional duties with unflagging mechanical precision, his heart was no longer in it as of yore.

He took an early opportunity of informing his colonel of the favourable turn his affairs had taken, and wrote Mildred a letter, the wording of which took him the best part of a Sunday afternoon.

Countess Szent Imre had gone to spend a fortnight at Pesth; so he was left for a time to his professional duties alone, and to his reflections concerning both the past and the future.

Great was his relief when, one day early in June, he received a note from the Countess announcing her return, and bidding him come and see her whenever he liked. The following day saw him rather earlier than usual at his work, hoping to bring it to a satisfactory conclusion by four p.m., and then to drive over to the castle. A life like George's, where the routine of successive days hardly varies and makes them pass with startling rapidity, soon produces the effect of losing account of time; and it was only on noticing the dates on the daily papers received just before leaving that George said to himself; "By Jove! I quite forgot it is the ninth—her wedding-day, of course!"

His face clouded over just for a moment, and involuntarily he looked back and thought how, not so very long ago, he had dreaded the vision of that day: and now, but for the merest chance, he would have let it pass unnoticed. He lit a cigarette, and going to his writing-table snatched up a telegraph form and wrote, with a hand that betrayed the emotion he felt:

COUNTESS OF DEVEREUX,
    88, Grosvenor Square, London, W.
Please accept my sincerest and most heartfelt wishes and congratulations.
                    GEORGE MANSFIELD.

In an unusually abrupt tone—for his manners to his inferiors were, as a rule, studiously considerate—he tells his servant to take the telegram to the post-office town, and then jumps into the pony-cart. His soldier servant does not display the alacrity in releasing the pony's head that suits his master's impatient temper. "Let him go, you fool!" he thunders; and, smartly touching up old Fobs, who rather resents such unaccustomed treatment, he rattles over the stony road at a pace that puts the springs to a some-

what severe test. The rapid motion suited him, and
the balmy spring breeze cooled his feverish brow.
Driving along the now so familiar avenue, he could
not but look back upon that wintry afternoon when,
in his sledge, he, for the first time, set out to find
his way to Kisfalva. He remembered it all: the
snowdrifts, his meeting with Father Vincent on his
way to a death-bed, and, above all, his first interview with Her.

Does a man pretty far "gone," as our friend
now was, become blind to Delilah's faults as a rule?
We doubt it. He would, of course, not admit them
to anybody else; but, in his innermost heart, he sees
the faults, knows them to be such, but loves her just
as much in spite of them, and would not remove
them had he the power to do so, for fear of marring
the harmony of the *ensemble*. Thus George, even
making the most liberal allowance for the wrongs the
Countess had suffered, could not but admit that many
an ill-natured epithet might be applied to her, not
wholly without a semblance of justification by sceptics,
or others, inclined to judge from appearances only,
but to him she was the impersonation of all that
makes woman tempting and bewitching—the lust of
the eye incarnate. The quiet, rather languid tones
of her voice, that smile so hard to interpret, those
glorious green eyes that would shine so brightly
when she was not too indolent to raise them from
underneath the thickly-fringed lids, had each and all
an altogether magic power over him.

He found the Countess lying in a hammock in

the garden, apparently so absorbed in reading as
hardly to notice his approaching footsteps. When
he was within a few yards of her, she looked up in-
dolently from her book and said:

"Oh, that is you, is it? I wasn't expecting you
until to-morrow; surely that was what I said, wasn't
it? Or have I made a mistake? I perpetually do;
but I really did not mean you to come to-day, for
my husband only returns from Pesth to-morrow morning. Anyhow, you must not stay and dine." She
burst out laughing merrily on seeing George's crestfallen look, the cause of which she pretended not to
understand. "Poor thing!" she said; "had it counter-
ordered its little supper at home, and is it afraid of
having to go to bed hungry? Well, then, it shall not;
though I have no doubt it will cost me my reputation. Only, seriously, I must turn you out the moment you have done dinner. Is that a bargain? And
if you are a good boy, you shall have a bottle of that
old Burgundy, which you say you don't often get in
our outlandish parts. *Now* are you happy?"

Of course George protested as to the purely dis-
interested character of his visit as far as the arrangement of his meals was concerned; but he could not
but admit to himself that the playful tone which the
Countess had adopted towards him was ill-suited
to his own frame of mind. For some occult reason,
or possibly for none at all, Countess Szent Imre was
that day in what she would herself have described
as "tearing spirits." (Foreigners who have mastered
the intricacies of our idiom are sometimes rather

given to overdo things, and to be *Anglis ipsis Angliores*
in the way of talking slang.) Thus she carried on
most of the conversation herself. Whence came her
lightheartedness? Did George want to know? She
hardly knew; nothing had happened to make her so;
perhaps it was the fine weather, perhaps the pleasure
of seeing him, perhaps anything else. And was it
not rather meritorious, her keeping up her spirits as
she did? Could anybody imagine a duller life? And
what could any of his friends at home say if they
were expected to do as she did?

Thus she rattled along lightly, touching first one
subject and then another. "How absurd it seems,"
she said, as the dinner bell rang, "that we should sit
down together in this ultra-conjugal fashion! I wonder
what the servants will think about it all; not that I
trouble my head much about them, or ever did, even
in old days."

Her face assumed a thoughtful expression, as it
mostly did when reminiscences of the past would rise
to her mind. Her thoughts were evidently wandering backwards, and her manner was absent throughout the rest of the dinner. Her injunctions to George
about leaving early had probably been wiped away
by the train of her thoughts; for the moon rising on
the horizon found him still in her company. The
gardens below the terrace upon which they were
standing, were beginning to show streaks of light,
making the shadow and darkness of the forests beyond
more gloomy and profound. Far in the distance,
the weird notes of a Tzigane band were just dis-

cernible, now rising to impassioned, heart-stirring notes, then again growing fainter and all but dying away.

"Come indoors," said the Countess; "I cannot bear the moonlight; it always did affect me. By the bye," she began, "do you remember my once telling you about a circus girl who played rather a prominent part in my early life?" Her voice, somehow, had not its wonted softness, and the rather abrupt manner in which she spoke betrayed the extreme tension of her nerves. "She has done well for herself. I happened to hear from Paris to-day that she is the first *écuyère* at the Hippodrome, with a Russian prince smothering her in diamonds. Not bad, is it? But then, her early training was a good one—I don't mean as regards the *haute école*. After all, perhaps it is better as it is; nothing is worth caring for much, and 'Im Grabe ist Ruh.'"

George could discern her eyes getting moist as she spoke; but, as if with an endeavour to brush away the thoughts that were oppressing her and that caused her heart to throb in angry tumult, she said:

"How selfish I am; I have been talking of nothing but myself! Tell me now about your troubles. Has any day been fixed for the marriage?"

"The marriage is to-day; *she is married now.*"

"Are you very unhappy?" is the only reply, in tones scarcely audible; but he guesses the meaning from the working of the lips.

"Unhappy? You asked me the same question a few weeks ago. Had I told you the whole truth

then, I should have said I did not think I could live
through the day. *Now*, the Past is effaced; *now*,
my happiness lies in these little tiny hands." He
seizes them and kisses them passionately. "Your
frowns alone can make me unhappy, and I would sell
my soul for one of your sweet smiles, for one look
from those green eyes I love. I know I never can
wipe out the past with you; I know I never can take
the place in your heart which *he* had. But, say, do
you think you do care for me—just one little bit?"

The long restrained passion is fast gaining mastery
over him; her eyes are veiled by the drooping lids;
her lips barely part to faintly utter: "Should you be
here if I did not?" and they do nothing to escape
meeting his.

As George Mansfield drove away that evening, he
stopped his pony on passing the front of the house
under the terrace where, bathed in the moonlight,
stood the tall and stately figure he had clasped in
his arms. Not a sound was to be heard around the
vast, silent, gloomy mansion. He just caught the
words "Good bye, darling!" from the lips that blew
him a parting kiss.

Vanity or self-love had no share in the feeling of
joy, so intense as not to be experienced twice in a
lifetime, that filled George's heart to overflowing during that midnight drive through the Hungarian Puszta.
Should death overtake him there and then, he would
not look upon his life as wasted. He had won the
love of the woman whose vision was always before
him as the incarnation of all that is lovely and seduc-

live; of all that is noble and good. True, she had sinned in her early days; but did not the very frankness of her confession wipe away the stain, and was she not now his, and only his?

A clock in a neighbouring village struck twelve, and as he counted the strokes, slowly following each other at long-drawn intervals, the thought flashed across him that the moon that had all but shone upon the sealing of the unholy bond consecrated that evening, was the honeymoon of her to whom he had once plighted his troth. He shrugged his shoulders at the thought.

His pony, anxious to return to home comforts, was going freely up to his bit, and was, no doubt, rather aggrieved at having his progress suddenly checked without any reason that he could detect; for, passing over a little wooden bridge which crossed a brook swollen by the recent rains, George pulled up short. He took out his watch, and severed from its chain the ring Mildred had given him before they parted. One moment afterwards it had disappeared in the angry torrent. "Farewell to the past!" were his only words.

*   *   *   *   *

That same day, the well-known strains of Mendelssohn's Wedding March pealed forth to a "large and fashionable" assembly gathered together at St. Peter's, Eaton Square, to see Mildred Charteris wedded to Lord Devereux. Hers was not the nature to turn back from the decision she had come to, under the impression—be it justified or not—that the obligation

she was under to Lord Devereux for his spontaneous
act of generosity could be cancelled but in one way.
Her stern and unrelenting sense of duty never allowed
her to waver in the accomplishment of what was little
less than an act of self-immolation.

The whole truth was known by nobody save Mrs.
Garrard, to whom she felt a steadily growing attach-
ment. Needless to say, Mrs. Jack Arthur appeared
at the wedding in her very smartest attire. She
thoroughly approved of the arrangement, and credited
herself with having materially contributed to the accomplishment of it.

The solemn words "I will" have been spoken
and the rings exchanged. A general feeling of relief
is prevalent that it is all "safely over," and people
are looking for their carriages, with feelings divided
between the wish of seeing the wedding presents
and misgivings at to sacrificing their luncheon by so
doing.

To adopt the style of the society chroniclers, we
will but add that in the afternoon Lord and Lady
Devereux left for Staplemoor Park, his lordship's
country seat in Leicestershire for the honeymoon.

CHAPTER XIV.

"I will be quiet and talk with you,
And reason why you are wrong;
You wanted my love—is that much true?
And so I did love, so I do:
What has come of it all along?

Oh, Love, Love, no, Love! not so indeed!
You were just weak earth, I knew;
With much in you waste, with many a weed
And plenty of passions run to seed,
But a little good grain, too."

ROBERT BROWNING.

A FEW months have gone by; the leaves are falling rapidly under the angry blasts of the autumnal
gales; people are beginning to talk over their plans
for the winter and the prospects of the forthcoming
hunting season. Mildred has settled down to her
new existence with cheerful resignation. She was
determined to fulfil all the duties of her position,
and before long the tenants on the large property,
as well as those in need, had learnt to appreciate
Lady Devereux's kind heart and the willingness with
which she lent her ear to their manifold grievances.
Thus, there was no lack of fresh occupations and
fresh subjects of interest in her life; perhaps the
social side of her duties was the one from which
she derived the least satisfaction. Lord Devereux

was too proud of his handsome young wife in any
way to restrain his naturally very hospitable instincts,
so that the spare rooms at Staplemoor were scarcely
ever empty. Mildred was far less acquainted with
all the little intricacies of society than her Lord; so
she hardly took more than a formal part in the
framing of the lists for the parties, rapidly succeed-
ing each other.

Mrs. Jack Arthur watched Mildred's first steps
in her new line of life with concentrated interest.
As a near country neighbour, and from having been,
at least in her own estimation, more or less in-
strumental to the making up of the marriage, she
felt herself justified in claiming a certain amount of
intimacy. Any illusion she might have had on this
score was speedily dispelled. Many reports concerning Mrs. Arthur, which Mildred had formerly taken
little heed of, or put down to mere ill-natured gossip,
had taken more consistency now that conversation in
her presence had grown less guarded; and she was
fully determined not to let Mrs. Jack become what
she described as a "tame cat" in the house. On
the other hand, her friendship for Mrs. Garrard went
on steadily progressing, She liked her fearless,
straightforward contempt of all the little conventional
shams and falsehoods, and her refreshing disregard
of the higher or lower social status of people about
whom she expressed an opinion.

The two friends were sitting together one morning
after breakfast, in Mildred's boudoir, a room pleasing
to the eye in its simplicity, and suggestive of a

thoroughly cultivated taste on the part of its owner. There was a sort of genuine look about everything the room contained, and a scrupulous avoidance of over decoration and repletion with the costly little knick-knacks of doubtful taste with which we see too many boudoirs crammed nowadays.

The last remnants of the week's party had just left. Lord Devereux's broad-shouldered form was seen vanishing down the avenue in his phaeton on his way to a county magistrates' meeting, so the two ladies felt sure of an undisturbed morning.

"Oh, what a comfort to have the place to ourselves at last; isn't it, Maggie?" says Mildred. "I don't think I could have stood another day of that little Lady St. Austin, with her curls and her simpering *minauderies*, and her sidling up to Captain Drummond. And when she turns up those languishing eyes to heaven, and talks about religion, and our duties towards the lower classes, and all that, I feel inclined to slap her. Much good the lower classes will learn from following her example. Now, I am going to read for half an hour, just to take the taste away whilst you are writing your letters; and then we will have a quiet talk."

"All right, dear child," says the other affectionately; "but if I were you I would not make myself unhappy about Lady St. Austin. She is a harmless little insect that flutters about in the sunshine, but that I should not think worthy of a second thought."

A pause of some duration ensues, during which

Mrs. Garrard's pen is hard at work. At last, Mildred looks up from her book, and says:

"I wonder what is the matter with Mrs. Arthur. I can see she can't bear me any longer. Have you any idea?"

"Is that all the benefit you have derived from reading about spiritual life, to worry yourself about what is going on underneath Mrs. Arthur's carroty curls? Of course she does not love you any more. She thought she had made your marriage, and was going to what the Americans call 'run the show' ever after. She finds out her mistake, and turns sulky in consequence; that's all. In fact, I should not be surprised if she were to try and let you feel it one day, if she gets the chance. However, don't let us waste our time talking about Mrs. Jack; we shall not get such an opportunity again in a hurry, and my letters can wait." She sits down close by her friend, whose hand she takes in her own: "Now, I want to talk about you, and you only. I am not going to ask you any questions that your father-confessor, if you had one, might ask; but anyhow, you can tell me this much: You don't regret anything, do you?"

"Regret! No," said Mildred, slowly and thoughtfully; "I suppose if it was to be done over again I should do the same thing. My object was to save George from going to the bad, if I possibly could do so. This, I trust, I have accomplished. Of course, Devereux only paid all this money for my sake, though he was too generous to say so. Nevertheless, to all intents and purposes, it was a bargain, and I have to fulfil my share of it. No; I am not what you call unhappy, though it is much more horrible being married to one man when you care for another than I ever thought. Devereux is very, very kind to me—far more so than I deserve; but I am sure he is already beginning to realise that I don't quite feel for him as I should, and that I never will. Poor George! I wonder if he will ever know the whole truth. How little he could have suspected all this when he told me—so long ago, it seems now—I had better marry 'Old Devereux,' as he called him."

In her appreciation of Mrs. Jack Arthur's feelings towards her friend, Mrs. Garrard had shown her quickness of perception. Mildred's rather reserved manner, and the want of alacrity with which she received many of Mrs. Jack's suggestions, had left a certain bitterness within the latter's mind, which was stimulated by her putting down a slight diminution of *empressement* in her friend Captain Atherstone's manner towards her, to the fascination exercised quite unconsciously upon him by the fair hostess of Staplemoor.

The time had been when slights and snubs had been her daily bread, and when she could not afford to resent them; but this was different now, and she was not going to stand the "airs" Lady Devereux might choose to give herself; for, had it not been for her, Mildred might still be withering away in some tumble-down old place in Hampshire.

Anyhow, if her ladyship was going to be nasty, she should soon learn that two could play at that game. Without having any very definite object in view, she thought it might very likely suit her purpose to obtain some information concerning George Mansfield's movements; and a far surer way of obtaining this appeared to her to apply for it to Colonel Greville, in Vienna, instead of writing to George himself. She had met the Colonel on and off, on various occasions in London, and, knowing as he did that George had been one of her "set," he could not think it in any way surprising that she should write to make inquiries about him. Besides, Mrs. Jack was a pretty good hand at writing letters without the recipient being any the wiser as to the particular object of her inquiries.

Before very long, Colonel Greville's answer reached her:

"With regard to George Mansfield, all I can say is that he is going well and strong. If he is broken-hearted he is a better hand at concealing his feelings than I ever gave him credit for. He does not often come up to Vienna; in fact, very seldom; but the report is, that he is going on anyhow with a most fascinating Hungarian countess. Of course, I cannot vouch for the truth of the report, but I am inclined to think there might be something in it. He talks vaguely of going home for a few weeks, later on; but I doubt his tearing himself away from Delilah just yet."

This was all Mrs. Jack wanted to know, and

she thought she saw her way towards having her little revenge.

An opportunity was not long in coming, for, dining one night at Staplemoor, somehow George Mansfield's name was mentioned in the course of conversation. Lord Devereux at once joined in:—

"Capital fellow, George; and sure to get on, from all I hear. Has anybody heard from him lately? The last news I had was that he was doing well, and was pretty hard-worked with the autumn manœuvres."

The subject might have dropped, had not Mrs. Jack Arthur, in rather a slow, deliberate tone, and closely watching the effect produced by her words on Mildred's face, said:

"I am so glad to have such a good account—of course, you never can believe half the things people tell you; but somehow I fancy I heard he had eloped with some lovely foreign countess, or, at any rate, was on the point of doing so. I was told the name, but I really could not even attempt to pronounce it."

Rather an awkward pause ensued, and involuntarily, though, perhaps, for not more than a second, everybody's eyes turned upon poor Mildred. Captain Atherstone at once came to the rescue; his devotion for Mrs. Jack had been cooling down of late, and he considered this last move of hers a downright shabby trick:

"Upon my soul! what a wonderful fountain of

information you are, Mrs. Jack! Why, Dalziel and the Central News put together are not in it with you! I wonder, though, where you got that last item from. But I don't care who it was, for I don't believe one word of it. George is the last man I know to do that sort of thing."

It was all that Mildred could do to refrain from showing, if only by a glance, her gratitude for Jim Atherstone's timely relief. The remark was probably shortly afterwards forgotten by most of those present; but the poisoned shaft had nevertheless struck home with Mildred. Even making allowance for a considerable amount of exaggeration on Mrs. Arthur's part, Lady Devereux could not credit her with having altogether invented the story; and, knowing George's weak nature and the temptations his life must expose him to, she could not but admit to herself that there was, at the very least, some sort of possibility in it.

And was it for this that she had sacrificed herself—merely to furnish George with the means of devoting himself to another woman, and of forgetting in her company every fond memory of the past? Was this the gratitude she had to expect from him? After very few moments of reflection, she came to a decision as to the course she would pursue. She felt it altogether beneath her to question Mrs. Arthur as to the source of her information, or as to any further particulars the latter might possess. She would address herself to George himself. Let him misinterpret her motives in doing so, if he chose; but she felt she had almost a right to know the truth.

It was only when she had taken up her pen that she realised the extreme difficulty and delicacy of the task before her. Nearly an hour had elapsed before she finally admitted her inability to improve upon the following missive:

My DEAR GEORGE,—You have often told me I am different from most other women. Perhaps I am in some points, one of which is that when I write with a particular purpose, I do not keep it for the end of my letter; nor do I add it on as a postscript, as if inspired with some after-thought. This letter has a purpose, and this is what it is:

I was told a day or two ago by a friend of yours —and I suppose I should say of mine—before a considerable number of people, that you were on the point of eloping with some foreign countess—if you had not done so already. You may say that you owe no account to anybody as to your actions, and that it is no business of mine. It is no business of mine as Mildred Charteris; but as Lady Devereux I feel bound to speak. Were it otherwise, you know me too well—whatever my feelings in the past may have been—to think I would stoop to question you, or to plead for the remembrance of a past, after all, not so very distant. You will, I trust, discard that notion, should it ever even present itself to your mind. You little know me if you entertain it.

The reason why I feel bound to write is, that I am most anxious Lord Devereux should be able to keep the regard, esteem and affection he had for you. I leave it to you to judge, whether this could be the case if you abandoned the profession which he has—I am bound to say, most generously—assisted, or rather enabled, you to remain in. To my mind, nothing that could have happened to you, had he not come to your assistance, could be much worse than the life you seem to be bent upon preparing for yourself.

I can but repeat, pray don't trouble to consider my feelings in the matter; but do not let me think you could ever forget what is due to yourself.

If there is no truth whatever in the report, tear up this letter and forget it was ever written. If I do not hear from you within a reasonable time, I suppose I shall know what conclusions to draw from it.

Good-bye!

Yours, very sincerely,

M. D.

In telling her friend, Mrs. Garrard, that she did not regret the step she had taken, Lady Devereux had, no doubt, spoken the truth, though she purposely understated the heavy burden which her sacrifice had imposed upon her.

Her health of late had not been quite what it used to be, and this also contributed to depress her spirits; and hard as she might struggle against it,

she felt herself slowly drifting into the part of the
femme incomprise. Lord Devereux, cheery, kind
hearted and easy-going, as he was, could not but, at
times, admit to himself that his handsome wife was
something of a white elephant to him; and his ab-
sences from home became more and more frequent.

CHAPTER XV.

"Whilst skies are blue and bright,
    Whilst flowers are gay;
Whilst eyes that change ere night
    Make glad the day;
Whilst yet the calm hours creep,
Dream thou—and from thy sleep
Then wake to weep."

SHELLEY.

IT is a common theme that does duty over and over again, Sunday after Sunday, from countless pulpits and in every intelligible idiom, that real happiness in this life is granted to the righteous only; and when we see the "children of the world," whose only law is the accomplishment of their own desires, flourishing and basking in the possession of all the good things this finite life can grant, we must not be taken in by appearances, but must look below the surface, etc., etc., that, to put it into homely language, there is a skeleton in every cupboard and so forth. The consensus of countless eminent theologians has established this as an axiom, though it might, with some fairness, be questioned whence the information is derived; since the "worldlings" who are depicted in such striking colours are not much given to seek the comfort of spiritual advisers or to make them their confidants, should the presence of the gnawing worm be temporarily felt beneath the glittering surface.

Be this as it may, the few months that followed the moonlit night at Kisfalva, when Countess Szent Imre had first listened to his passionate words of love, were to George a time of almost unalloyed and cloudless happiness.

His code of morals was at that time not very different from that of most young men. He was free —as far as Mildred was concerned—through her marriage. To entertain any lurking affection for her would, in fact, be far more guilty than to transfer his affections to Countess Szent Imre. These and similar sophisms did away with any feelings of self-reproach that would occasionally rise to his mind. His whole life was now entirely wrapped up in his new love. There was not a moment in the day when thoughts of her were not present in his mind. He consulted her about every action in his life; had she cared to do so, she could have seen every letter he received or wrote. He was in that stage when the lover's one wish appears to be to immolate his whole personality, his will, his judgment, his likes and dislikes, and to see them, so to speak, absorbed and assimilated by those of the woman at whose shrine he worships.

Needless to say, the response he met with was hardly tuned to the same pitch, and Countess Szent Imre's manner towards him was by no means effusive and outwardly very little, if at all, different from what it had been hitherto. At first this had caused considerable surprise and disappointment to George; especially when, seeing her again for the first time after he had confessed his passion for her, she greeted him in the self-same listless, rather *distrait* manner as before; but he was in the frame of mind in which he would have found an excuse for whatever she could have done.

Of Father Vincent he had begun to see less than previously. His subscriptions towards the hospital became more frequent in the measure in which his requests for the priest's company diminished. The latter carefully avoided anything that savoured of intrusion; he could not but know by public rumour of George's incessant visits to Kisfalva, the motive for which was palpable to less keen a student of human nature.

* * * * *

The threatening cloud that some years ago hung over a large part of the Continent seemed rather closer than usual to the bursting point during the summer of 188 —. There was some talk of the 24th Lancers being moved towards the frontier, and unusual activity prevailed in riding-school and drill-ground. Thus George's time was too much taken up with his professional duties for him to have much leisure, and sometimes a week would pass without his setting eyes on the lovely Countess. The eagle Saalburg, was upon him and eye of his captain, Prince his troop with even more than usual diligence; and as he felt sure that any shortcoming would no doubt be attributed to his close vicinity to the fascinations of Kisfalva, George was doubly anxious not to be found in fault. Thus he was seen one morning about 6 A.M. scanning his troop with an eye that had now grown thoroughly practised, before marching off to the drill-ground where the six squadrons were to work together, a force which, on the full war footing on which the Austrian Cavalry is permanently kept, is about equivalent to three regiments of ours.

A lovely autumn morning; a slight haze was gradually rising from the valleys, dispelled by the rays of the sun, shining brightly in spite of the early hour, and glistening on the lances and drawn swords of the men. George was prepared for a long and heavy morning's work, as the Colonel was to inspect the regiment; but he knew he would have the afternoon to himself, and his heart beat beneath his tunic at the thought of her with whom he hoped to spend it. One consideration only would now and then come across his mind to mar his spirit of perfect contentment. His first charger had cast a shoe the night before, and was not fit to come out, so he had to content himself with a half-broken mare, quiet enough when by herself, but rather nervous when at the head of a troop. Having about five miles to ride at foot's-pace to the drill-ground, he ordered his men to ride at ease, and, lighting a cigarette, he let his thoughts wander at their own free will.

He was riding alongside of his troop on the grass, enjoying the brisk morning air, and, judging from his countenance, his thoughts likewise were in harmony with the exhilariting influences that surrounded him. At any rate, he was so much absorbed in them that he did not at first notice the sound of horses' feet coming in the same direction and rapidly overtaking him. One glance showed him the familiar outline of Countess Szent Imre on her chestnut pony, cantering gaily up to him. He was startled out of his reverie, for the mere sight of her sent a thrill through him. Yes, it was she right enough; the delicate figure gracefully swaying to the motion of her pony; the rich auburn hair tightly coiled under a sailor's hat, which was trimmed with a ribbon of the colours in which George won a regimental steeplechase a month ago; her covert coat was opened, and the snowy shirt-front faintly indicated the beautiful outline of her figure. The fresh morning air and her brisk canter had brought a brighter colour than usual to her face, and her eyes were sparkling with more than accustomed animation.

"Good morning, Lord George," she greets him, as she pulls up. "I was told the Colonel was going to give you a real old-fashioned field day this morning, so I curtailed my slumbers to admire you all in your martial splendour. What is that you are riding?"

"She's only a four-year-old. I have hardly ever had her out yet, for she caught influenza the moment I got her. She is a nice one to look at, isn't she? But this is indeed a treat, seeing you out at this unearthly hour! Have you taken to somnambulism, or does your conscience keep you from sleeping?"

"No, it is not that; though," dropping her voice, "if it was, it isn't for you to remind me of it. But don't imagine I have come out to see *you,* for I really am very fond of soldiering, and the Colonel sent me a note asking me to come out."

"Oh, he did, did he? He did not tell you by any chance how long he was going to keep us out?"

"Very long, I fancy," says she, with a provoking smile; "and anyhow you will be much too exhausted to come over to Kisfalva in the afternoon. But here we are; I can see the Colonel now. Oughtn't you to salute or do something?"

"All right," says George. "You had better keep a bit more to the left, for I am going to let them form into line," and he rings out the word of command.

Not the oldest veterans could have carried out the movement—a simple one, no doubt—with more mathematical precision than did George's troop, one third of which consisted of mere boys who had only joined eight or nine months before. Having formed into line, he took his place in the squadron, and then cantered off to where the Captain was to give him the usual report. In so doing he could not but have some slight misgivings as to his mount's likely behaviour during the course of the day, for the mare was fighting for her head, and he had some little difficulty in pulling up short in front of Prince Saalburg in order to salute and to utter the usual formula: "Herr Rittmeister, ich melde gehorsamst den zweiten Zug, zweiunddreiszig Reiter, keine Hand-pferde."

The Colonel arrived shortly afterwards and in-spected the regiment in every detail; first every troop singly and then in squadron line. The 6th squadron, to which George belonged, took its turn after all the others; and after a few movements had been gone through the order to halt and dismount was given. The Colonel then sent for the officers of the squad-rons and expressed his satisfaction with what he had seen. He now proposed going through an exer-cise which, though not frequently practised in time of peace, nevertheless forms part of the regimental drill, and may be required in warfare.

Supposing a regiment should be attacked by sur-prise when in bivouac and the horses picketed, one squadron would be ordered to bridle at once and to mount barebacked, in order to give the rest of the force time and cover to saddle and turn out. The sixth squadron would now unsaddle and mount on the bugle call of "Alarm" being sounded, and would advance against a marked enemy.

The officers rode back to their squadrons. Prince Saalburg gave the order to unsaddle, together with a few instructions as to keeping distances, and to the manner in which the rear rank should hold their lances which, in the case of a man's seat getting unsteady, are apt to prove more dangerous to the front rank than to the enemy. The Captain is de-lighted that his squadron should have been selected for what is considered rather a show performance.

Quite incidentally he suggests to George tightening his curb-chain a link or two, and adds: "I hope you will be able to hold that mare; for remember you are leading the second troop, and the whole squadron goes by you. If you come closer up to me than the thirty-two paces prescribed by regulations, of course the squadron must follow."

George frankly admits to himself that he does not quite like the duty he is about to perform, as he is well aware that in the event of his steed becoming at all unmanageable, any vagaries of his might spoil the entire effect of the movement to be carried out by the squadron. A hot-tempered and ill-furnished thoroughbred is an awkward conveyance both to sit and to steer bare-backed with a drawn sword, doubly so with the knowledge that any deviation from the direction given, or any acceleration of speed must be followed by some hundred and fifty horses following behind. If only George had his old charger, he would have enjoyed the fun as much as anybody; but under the circumstances he rather dreaded making a fool of himself under the eyes of his colonel — and another. Whilst the squadron had unsaddled and picketed, the marked enemy had been told off, with orders to emerge from the cover of a rather sparsely grown plantation of beeches about three-quarters of a mile from where the squadron had halted. The ground rose in a gentle slope, beautiful turf throughout, uninterrupted by anything save occasionally a few rabbit holes.

At last the sharp, shrill note from the silver

trumpet is heard, followed instantly by the order to
bridle and mount. No time is lost in removing the
pickets—the head ropes only being undone and the
bridles slipped over the halters; there is no con-
fusion and very little noise. The favourite anathema
of "Psia krew!" is occasionally heard in guttural
tones, when the first attempt at mounting a charger
who persistently sidles away has proved abortive; but
in an incredibly short time every man is in his place,
and the squadron has formed into line, Prince Saalburg galloping through in between the two centre
troops just as they are forming; and without waiting
for his trumpeter, he rings out the word of command
to advance at a trot, indicating the direction of the
marked enemy's approach.

George was on the mare's back at the very first
sound of the bugle-call, and his voice is heard in
quick, sharp tones getting his men into line. This
is soon done, and he takes up his position at their
head, the squadron advancing in line at a brisk trot.
As soon as the "skeleton" of the approaching enemy
becomes more clearly defined, the word of command
"Gallop!" is given. It is by no means the pleasantest
sensation imaginable having a line of cavalry immediately at one's heels, each man of which is armed
with a lance which describes rather alarming gyra-
tions, when the right hand is brought down to assist
the bridle-hand, which will soon become necessary
owing to the unavoidably unsteady seat on a bare-
backed horse; and the squadron now advancing at a
gallop in no wise showed the unbroken line it did

under ordinary circumstances, nor was the same absolute silence maintained in the ranks.

George, at first, was fairly taken aback at the good behaviour of his second charger. On breaking into a gallop she no doubt threw up her head, fighting to get it free, and made a rather wild bound forward; but his light hands steadied her, and though she was no doubt pulling a bit, he was well able to keep at the regulation distance from the squadron-leader. George was beginning to congratulate himself, but it was too good to last. The men representing the enemy had orders to approach within sixty or seventy yards of the advancing squadron, when the order to charge would be given, and they would turn back and ride off. As the word "Charge!" was shouted by Prince Saalburg, and as the deafening cheers rose from the ranks, every man and every horse struggling for the foremost place, the mare made a dart forward, and, by an effort that almost pulled George over her neck, she got her head free, and in another second her rider knew that she had got entirely beyond his control. He shot past his squadron-leader, who was then about to have the call to rally sounded, and soon was well clear of the squadron. He did not lose his presence of mind, knowing full well that in the terror-stricken state the mare was in, it would be merely wasting his strength to attempt to stop her there and then. She was making straight for the direction whence the marked enemy had emerged. The distance that separated him from the little group of trees was diminishing at an alarming rate; so George thought it wisest to reserve his strength in order to steer clear of the overhanging boughs. The mare, to whom the scabbard beating her flanks was an additional source of terror, showed no signs of slackening speed. Her head was well up in the air, with her clenched teeth tightly set on the bit.

George remembered having heard that the ground beyond the beeches was rough and stony and full of rabbit holes, and he began to wonder what he had best do. His position struck him as a ludicrous rather than a dangerous one; anyhow he had the satisfaction of knowing that the misbehaviour of his mount had not in any way interfered with the complete success of the movement executed by the squadron. He guessed that many eyes must be fixed upon him with amusement, if not with anxiety, for which there was not much apparent cause. Of course, it would have been very easy for him to let himself slip off the mare; but, firstly, he did not like to run the risk of her breaking her knees galloping riderless over the rough stony ground; and, secondly, he did not fancy the prospect of trudging back the best part of a mile on foot to where the Colonel and Countess Szent Imre were posted. Had *she* not been there, it might have been different; but his courage failed at the idea of facing her possible sarcasms. She had taken her place at the Colonel's side, and the latter explained to her the movements of the squadron, which was then rallying and returning at a trot to its former position. Her eyes were fixed on George's wild career, with a look more of interest than of concern. Once only she turned to Count Wartenstein: "What is there beyond those trees, supposing he is not able to pull up before?"

"A nasty bit of rough, stony ground, full of holes; but if he can keep this side of the trees and bear to the left, he will be all right."

The Colonel has taken out his field-glasses and is watching intently. He seems to be making straight for the trees," he now says, speaking more to himself than to his companion; "I can see that animal with its head high up in the air worse than ever —— My God! what a nasty fall! She has rolled right over him! Welinski!"—this is to the regimental surgeon, who is standing by the dismounted regiment —"jump up and ride off over there. I am afraid he is hurt; I can't see him move. Come with me!" —this to Countess Szent Imre, and he gallops off to where George was lying.

Feeling the mare tearing down the incline that led to the clump of beeches at a madder pace than ever, George now rallies whatever strength he has left to make his supreme effort, and to pull her over to the left clear of the trees. He just succeeds in doing this; but the ground right round the little plantation is burrowed out by rabbits. He bent forward to avoid coming in contact with an overhanging bough. It was the last thing he remembered doing, for not the tenth part of a second afterwards, the mare came down as if she had been shot, going head over heels, to remain lying motionless over the nether limbs of her luckless rider.

Hurrying her pony along in the wake of Count Wartenstein's charger, Countess Szent Imre galloped up to the spot where George lay. Her face was of a deadly pallor, but her self-possession never left her for a moment. The surgeon and one or two of the officers had reached the spot just before her, and had extricated him from underneath the mare, who lay apparently as lifeless as her rider. Countess Szent Imre was off her pony almost before she had pulled up. With the exception of a very slight graze on the forehead, there were no external indications of any injury.

"What do you suppose it is?" Countess Szent Imre addressed the surgeon in a quick, abrupt tone; "concussion of the brain? I have a drop of port in my flask if that can do any good."

The surgeon did not answer; he had unbuttoned George's tunic and was endeavouring to feel the action of the heart. His face wore a very grave expression, and once or twice he shook his head as if speaking to himself.

The mid-day sun was beating down on the group that had collected round the man who, judging by all appearances, was breathing his last. His head was resting on a pillow improvised out of a cloak rolled over a saddle. With his ear pressed closely upon the breast of the reclining figure, the surgeon leant over him, an anxious look upon his honest, sunburnt face. In a semi-circle around stood, in the silence of suspense, his brother officers, watching every expression upon the surgeon's countenance; and just clear of the others, alongside the Colonel, was the tall, graceful figure of the Countess, her face white as a sheet, but only the very faintest motion of her lips betrayed the tension of her nerves. Far in the background, upon the brow of the slightly rising ground, the long extended line of the dismounted regiment stood out in bold relief against the horizon.

The suspense was intolerable to all present, when at last, with a sigh of relief, the surgeon spoke: "I can just detect the action of the heart, but it is very feeble; of course there is severe concussion of the brain, and the right wrist is broken. I cannot yet tell for certain about the spine."

The verdict having been pronounced, Count Wartenstein, who shrewdly suspected the state of things existing between his young subaltern and the lovely woman who was standing by his side, thought it his duty to spare her nerves too severe a test. He therefore turned to her with an air of some authority: "I do not think there can be any cause for immediate anxiety; I have seen hundreds of cases of concussion of the brain quite as bad as this without any fatal result; but, Countess, this is no place for you. I have sent for an ambulance waggon which will be here directly to take him home. Please don't stay any longer."

She saw the kind intention which the stern tone of his voice could not disguise, and was proportionately grateful; for she felt the tension was so great that she must soon break down; and, only adding, with a voice to which she endeavoured hard to give firmness, that she would inquire in the afternoon, she let the Colonel put her on her pony. Her shortest way home took her across the exercise ground where the dismounted regiment was halted, and as she cantered past the line, the dull, expressionless countenances lighted up just for a moment, one by one, suggestive of the effect produced by a spark falling on the train of gunpowder; and with a guttural murmur of admiration their eyes followed the dainty figure rapidly receding.

Once out of sight and hearing, Countess Szent Imre pulled up her pony: nature refused to be ruled any longer by her iron will, and she burst into a fit of passionate sobbing.

CHAPTER XVI.

" With eloquence innate his tongue was armed,
Though harsh the precept yet the people charmed;
For, letting down the golden chain from high,
He drew his audience upwards to the sky."

JOHN DRYDEN.

AFTER the Countess had left, they examined the exact spot where the accident had happened. The mare had got her off leg, well over the fetlock, into a rabbit-hole, which caught it like a trap. The joint was broken, and a merciful bullet put an end to the poor animal's sufferings. The ambulance waggon was on the spot very soon afterwards, and George, still utterly unconscious of all that was going on around him, was conveyed home.

For three days and nights he remained in a state of stupor, unaware of the anxious glances exchanged around his bedside, and of the subdued whispers in which every fresh symptom was discussed and analysed. One of the luminaries of the medical profession in Vienna had been summoned at the wish of his colonel, and it had at last been ascertained that the skull was not fractured, and that there was no injury to the spine. The concussion of the brain was obviously of an exceptionally severe character,

and the fracture of the right wrist a most compli-
cated one.

Absolute quiet in the sick-room being one of the
most stringent injunctions of the doctor, it was not
difficult for Countess Szent Imre to come in at times
when she was sure of meeting nobody but the nurse
who attended the invalid and whose discretion she
could rely upon. Her husband had gone for his
annual cure to Carlsbad. Besides, she had by letter
applied for his consent to her visiting what appeared
to all intents and purposes to be a dying man.

It is the evening of the third day after the accident. The dim reflection of a shaded reading-lamp
lights up one side of her face, bringing into bold
relief the soft outline of her profile. Her expression
is more that of a sick nurse—tender, watchful and
attentive to every symptom—than that of the broken-
hearted woman sitting by her lover's bedside. In her
low, musical voice, the softness of which makes every
utterance from her fall upon the ear like words of
endearment, she addresses the nurse in her own
language:

"What did the doctor say this morning?"

With the volubility of her race the reply is given
that there are symptoms of consciousness returning
before long—such as increased restlessness and a
rise in the temperature. The doctor would call again
late in the evening. The Countess thereupon decided to wait until his arrival. She sat down in the
most comfortable armchair she could find and looked
around.

Beyond the narrow zone of light immediately
surrounding the lamp, the rest of the room was
buried in semi-obscurity, intensified by the gloomy
effect of the heavy oak rafters that formed the frame-
work of the ceiling. The plain deal boards of the
floor were only partially covered by Persian rugs
scattered about here and there. Coloured prints,
arms and sporting trophies enlivened the dulness of
the common, whitewashed walls; and on the ponder-
ous oak writing-table the Countess perceived a
coloured miniature of herself, done from a life-size
portrait in the boudoir where George saw her for the
first time.

While the nurse was absent preparing some
medicine the Countess took up the invalid's hand
and felt the feeble pulse. There were a few symptoms perceptible of returning life. The complete
stupor of the preceding days was gradually making
way to an increased restlessness, and the lips occasionally parted for some half-muttered, unintelligible
words.

The reflection that in all probability, should a
state of delirium set in, George's first words would
betray the state of his relations to her did not weigh
heavily on the Countess's mind, for the thought of
"what the world will say" did not rank high among
her cares. As another relapse to the previous
comatose state set in, she leant back in her chair,
and, half-closing her eyes, allowed her thoughts to
wander.

By what strange freak of destiny had it been

ordained that this boy should cross her path, and should be called upon to play a part in her existence? It all came back to her memory: the day she had first made his acquaintance, the growing intimacy and sympathy between them, and finally that moonlit night with the Tziganes playing in the distance. And looking now upon the shattered frame that lay in the narrow little bed close to her, the words of warning she had addressed to him came back to her mind the warning not to bestow upon her a feeling she was unable to return. She would willingly have made any sacrifice for him; would have nursed him with incessant care and devotion; but, in spite of all, how different it all was from what she had felt in old, bygone days!

And why had she allowed herself to drift further and further onward? What right had she to take into her keeping this boy's mind and soul and conscience, when she had so little to give in return? And, supposing he recovered, as she felt confident he would, should she once more tell him the whole truth, and sever the link that bound them together? Or were things to go on again as they had been, until, in her weariness, she cast him off? She shrugged her stately shoulders as if in doubt, perhaps almost in a state of gloomy indifference; and a fugitive smile flitted over her countenance as the cynical old adage flitted through her mind: "Le temps fait passer l'amour, et l'amour fait passer le temps."

She was thus musing, with her eyes half closed, letting her thoughts wander at their own will, when

a slight knock at the door interrupted her meditations, but it was only when it was gently opened to
admit Father Vincent that she languidly turned her
head. There was not the slightest trace of embarrassment or self-consciousness in her manner when
she rose to greet the priest; she had met him before
now at various bedsides, and her eyes made no attempt to avoid his earnest and almost reproachful
glance.

"Perhaps you are surprised at meeting me here,
Father Vincent," she began; "but your mission and
mine need in no way interfere with each other; conventionalism ceases on the threshold of the sick-
room, and we meet here in our common anxiety for
the welfare of a poor sufferer."

Nothing could be more natural and self-possessed
than the manner in which these words were uttered,
Countess Szent Imre at the same time holding out
her hand to the monk. Embarrassment and hesitation were painfully visible on the pale and worn
countenance of the latter. His fingers just met the
proffered hand without closing round it; and it was
only after a few seconds of reflection that he put
into words the thoughts that were so palpably before
his mind.

"Yes, Countess, we have indeed met before now
at the bedside of many a poor suffering creature, and
your charity is well known for miles around. To-
day, however, the circumstances appear to me different.
It is no part of my duties, nor have I any right, to
inquire into the motives that brought you here. I

know nothing about the social conventionalities you refer to, nor whether your presence here is in accordance with them or not. I cannot agree with you, however, when you say your mission and mine need not clash. Should my services be required, they will be proffered only too willingly at any time. For the present, you will excuse me if I withdraw."

All trace of shyness and embarrassment had now vanished from the priest's manner; the pale countenance was lighted up by a look of intense and fervent emotion, and the dark eyes shone like coals through the semi-obscurity of the room. He had drawn himself up to his full height; the folds of his dark brown cowl falling loosely round the spare, angular figure. The Countess had resumed her seat; her eyes were fixed upon the ground, as if studying the outline of the highly-varnished little boot that appeared from underneath her skirt; she listened apparently with languid interest, but without betraying the faintest emotion. Without raising her eyes she answered:

"Of course you will use your own discretion as to remaining here or not, As I was not aware I should have the advantage of meeting you here, I could not truthfully say that your arrangements will in any way affect mine."

The monk, after giving a glance to the bed where the invalid lay, utterly unconscious of what was taking place around him, was half through the door, when—like a true woman—she called him back. No prouder woman ever breathed than Countess Ilona Szent Imre; yet the look that shone forth from those deep eyes was one more of curiosity and interest than of wounded pride.

"Father Vincent," she began, "do you realise that your last words to me convey little short of a direct insult, such as no living man has ever dared address to me? I will not ask you what grounds you have for speaking in that manner: I will make your task easier, and will say the words that are on your lips. You have heard reports about me and the man who is lying here; you have, I dare say, been told I was his mistress. Supposing it were true, would you wish me to leave him to die here alone and friendless? Are those the precepts of the religion of charity and mercy that you profess to teach?"

She had risen to her feet, and stood defiantly facing the priest—the very incarnation of all that is alluring, of all that has stirred man's heart since the days of the Fall, be it to deeds of chivalry and valour, or to felony and vice. Unwillingly the priest relaxed his grasp of the door. A life of privation and self-abnegation had extinguished in him every vestige of passion; and his voice was now as calm, addressing the lovely woman who stood before him, as it would have been during the exercise of any of his ecclesiastical duties. Slowly and deliberately the words fell from his lips:

"I am not here to judge anyone's actions; I have not the right to do so, had I the wish. My motive for not wishing to remain here you have yourself mentioned: my mission is to visit the sick who are left friendless and alone, not those who are visited by ——" He checked himself abruptly.

"Pray go on," the Countess interrupted, her eyes just for one moment sending forth a flash of lightning; "this is most exciting. I gather that the moral atmosphere of this room is so vitiated by my presence that your sanctity might suffer from the contamination. I doubt your speaking with quite so much freedom were Lord George not lying here as inanimate as a corpse; *now*, of course, you are perfectly safe."

The bitter taunt had scarcely passed her lips ere she regretted it. The pallor on the monk's face took an even more livid hue, but there was no faltering in his voice when he replied:

"Forgive me, Countess, but it was you who forced this conversation upon me, which I would have done much to avoid. You tell me *fear* would close my lips. What does life offer to me that I should cling to it, do you suppose? or why should I look upon death, did it threaten me, as anything but a welcome release? But no more of these angry words; I do not presume to interfere or to find fault with the path you have chosen in life; let me go mine." And once more he moved towards the door.

"One moment, Father Vincent," she resumed— her voice had returned to its soft and almost pleading tone—"I do not wish to part from you in anger. My last words were unworthy of me; forget them. I don't trouble much about people's opinions concerning myself; but I should be sorry did you think more harshly of me than I deserve. What do you know of me? What the idle gossip-mongers of a little village choose to repeat to each other. You know nothing of my life, my surroundings, the temptations that beset me. Supposing I were to this poor boy all that you imply I am; is it nothing, according to you, that a woman's influence should watch over him, should incessantly strive to rouse and develop every good and noble sentiment within him; that she should use his affection towards her as a safeguard to himself against all that is lowering and debasing and degrading? Does that count for nothing in your eyes?

After a moment's hesitation the priest replied:

"Forgive me, Countess, if I cannot enter into these intricacies. I dare say you may be right from the point of view of the world you live in. My code is a simpler one; it teaches me that wrong remains wrong even if done with the problematical chance of doing good thereby, or rather of avoiding other evils. I know that falsehood and treachery, when committed to screen a woman's name, become actions of chivalry and almost of self-abnegation; are they for that less deteriorating to a man's nature? This boy, as you call him; why, any child would see that he is the very soul of honour and loyalty and truth. Now, not a day passes without his telling countless falsehoods—his very life is made up of them—and this is what you call rousing his nobler sentiments!

"I am deeply attached to him; do you suppose

I do not notice how gradually, from day to day, his whole nature is becoming warped and poisoned by the hourly practising of the art of deceit? Whose influence do you imagine that is due to, if not yours? He is now stricken down, perhaps never to recover. Should he do so, is it too much to expect from a nature, noble and generous as yours is, that you will let that baneful influence cease; that you will cast to the winds all that petty casuistry which least of all you believe in yourself, and that you will, by an act of renunciation, prove yourself superior to what you would fain make me believe you are?"

The fervour of deep and heartfelt conviction now lighted up the monk's countenance, and gave a power to his utterances hardly warranted by the simplicity of his words, pronounced with bated breath, so as not to disturb the slumber of the invalid.

The Countess listened to the end in deep silence, never raising her eyes from the ground. When he had done speaking, she rose and held out her hand.

"I will bear your words in mind, Father Vincent. It is a pity there are not more priests like you. The doctor will be here in a very few minutes; so my presence can be of no use. Good night! Much of what you say is true, though I trust not all."

She left the room; and two big tears shone in her eyes as she passed through the door, which the priest respectfully held open for her.

*   *   *   *   *   *

George's splendid constitution, assisted by the great medical skill which was placed at his disposal, enabled him to pull through. The return of consciousness brought with it attacks of high fever and delirium, during which he was watched with incessant care and devotion by the Franciscan monk. Night after night the latter would tell the nurse she might retire, and he would remain at George's bedside; and somehow the soothing effect of the serene, placid countenance of the priest, devoting himself to the self-imposed labour of love with unsurpassed zeal and judgment seldom failed to assert itself.

The invalid's face would suddenly brighten up when he saw the monk returning to his room, for no one else seemed to understand his wishes as he did; and on awakening in the morning his eyes would search in the dim light for the figure of Father Vincent.

Countess Szent Imre's visits were but scarce, once the critical stage was passed; the priest's words had come apparently to strengthen a resolution which until then had taken no definite shape, but which was now gaining a deeper hold upon her from day to day.

Months must necessarily elapse before George would be able to resume his military duties, chiefly on account of the difficulty he had in using the fractured wrist; and he had already sent in an application for six months' sick leave. On a chill, dreary afternoon in November he once more betook himself to Kisfalva to take leave of the Countess a day or two before his departure.

He was looking thin and worn, and as he approached the castle he smiled rather sadly, thinking within himself that very likely he would never again see those battlements that frowned over the archway which now resounded with the echoes of his pony's footsteps.

He found the Countess in her boudoir. A look of intense weariness and depression was upon the noble features that George now gazed at again after so long a time, and he fancied he saw tears glistening in her eyes. She greeted him warmly, but not effusively: and, after inquiring fully into the state of his health, she said:

"You find me in the depth of woes to-day and thoroughly out of liking with life. I have not been well, either, lately, and your departure is a very real additional grief to me. It is far better though, as it is, believe me. I have been thinking a great deal about it of late; Fate or Providence has decreed that this unfortunate accident of yours should be a landmark in the lives of both of us. I had intended that, even had you not decided upon leaving immediately, the past should be buried between us; but this will make it so much easier. Forgive me; I really have not the strength to wade through all the commonplaces usual on such occasions, as to meeting again as friends, and all that sort of thing; though I devoutly hope we shall. But somehow the beginning of our—friendship was not conventional, was it? so let the end be worthy of the beginning. I suppose I ought to say you will soon forget me. I don't, for I don't believe you will, or that you will be in the humour to say just yet: 'Lightly won, and lightly lost; a fair good-night to thee.' Shall you —darling?"

The airy, rather flippant tone in which she had begun speaking had gradually given way to an intonation far more in keeping with the expression of her face; and in the final question had melted into the softest tones of passionate endearment.

"You must not mind me," she added, no longer able to conceal the big tears gathering in her eyes; "somehow I am not myself to-day, and my nerves are out of order just now."

Alas for women's inconsistency and the frailty of their resolutions! Let soured spinsters shrug their angular shoulders and throw this book away in high dudgeon—should they not have done so before now —the truth must be told; and the leave-taking of Countess Szent Imre and her lover was very much what that of other lovers is.

Refine human passion, distil it, spiritualise it, ennoble it as you will with every attribute of the cultured soul and intellect; it alters it but little in the end.

CHAPTER XVII.

"Alas! I have nor hope, nor health,
   Nor peace within, nor calm around;
Nor that content, surpassing wealth,
   The sage in meditation found."

THOROUGHLY selfish though Lord Errington's nature was, it must not be supposed that the news of
George's accident and of his impending return home
left him altogether unimpressed. His intellectual
faculties were in no respect above the average, and
his brain was not wont to work at any very high
rate of speed; nevertheless, on certain occasions it
could be roused to a somewhat remarkable quickness of perception, and that was in gauging to what
extent any communication received about another
person would affect himself, his purse or his con-
venience. The practice of many years had given
him an almost unerring judgment in that respect.
The spontaneousness of warmer-hearted natures was
denied him; but once having accurately ascertained
in his own mind to what extent the misfortunes of
others could affect him, he was by no means incapable of a kind or even, apparently, a generous
action.

Thus, on hearing of his brother's accident, two
thoughts flashed across his mind all but simul-

taneously: firstly, a feeling of real and genuine anxiety, and the fervent wish for his recovery; secondly, the reflection that supposing George were invalided home, the burden of his maintenance would in all probability fall upon himself. But his better nature speedily asserted itself, and he wired out to Hungary to express his willingness to come and nurse his brother, should there be any urgent necessity for so doing. He was much relieved when a reply was received, signed by George, but written by the Countess, who well knew how little comfort the invalid would derive from his brother's company, gratefully declining the offer.

However, when he was informed of George's returning home on prolonged sick leave, he felt the moment had come when he must hold forth a helping hand. A small farm on one of his extensive Leicestershire properties happened to be tenantless just then, so he thought it could not do much harm to let George try his hand in the capacity of gentleman farmer, under the close supervision of a trusted bailiff. Anyhow, this would give George a semblance of an occupation, and would keep him out of mischief, the latter being intimately associated in Lord Errington's mind with life in town. That the farm he was putting at his brother's disposal lay within a few miles from Lord Devereux's country seat, and that this close vicinity might not be altogether free from objections, never even entered his mind.

Thus it came to pass that not many weeks after

George had taken leave of his regiment, for the time at least, he was settled at "The Folly," deeply interested in the selling of young stock and the manifold other pursuits of the gentleman farmer. Though apparently entirely restored to health—with the exception of the stiffness of his wrist, which caused him some anxiety—he was, nevertheless, in most respects, an altered man. All interest in life seemed somehow to have become extinct within him; he showed an amount of perseverance in picking up the necessary knowledge of farming that fairly took the old bailiff by surprise, but, otherwise, he was perfectly content to spend his evenings at home, though, needless to say, the doors of country houses would have been thrown open to the prodigal son on his home-coming, had he felt disposed to enter them.

He would sit sometimes for hours after dinner, buried in thought, with a listless, despondent look on his face, as if the mainspring of his vitality had gone out of order and had stopped working. Soon after his arrival at "The Folly," he had ascertained that Lord and Lady Devereux were not expected to come back from Scotland for some weeks; but even that communication failed to rouse him out of his languor.

Mrs. Jack Arthur was still on her annual trip abroad, and the other neighbours were comparative strangers to him, so there was no occasion for him to give up his habits of solitude. He was himself surprised to notice how little the prospect of meeting Mildred again affected him. So much had taken place since they had parted that it seemed hard to him to realise what a part she had once played in his life.

In the soft, mellow tints of that glorious painting, which may ere long grace the walls of some American plutocrat's mansion, Titian has contrasted, in a subtle allegory, Love—Sacred and Profane. There was not much of the divine spark in the passion which had enthralled George's entire nature; there was scarcely a vestige in it of that almost sacred feeling all but too noble for the weak human clay that shelters it. His love was sensual; not in the meaning of the word to which some odium must necessarily be attached, but merely inasmuch as all his senses had gradually been enthralled, bewitched and subjugated.

Any doubts he might have had as to the future footing on which he and the Countess Szent Imre might meet again were removed by a letter he received from her shortly after his return to England. She wound up with the words: "Do not imagine that because I once failed in my resolutions, I am likely ever to do so again. The past is dead and buried; try to forget me."

A few weeks after his arrival at Folly Farm, he heard from his bailiff that the inmates of Staplemoor were expected back within the next few days. The communication gave but little satisfaction to George; for different reasons, he, if anything, rather dreaded his first meeting with both of them, and anything that disturbed the groove of his quiet, emotionless existence was to him the reverse of welcome. However, he would comfort himself by thinking it was bound to happen, sooner or later, so there was no use fretting about it.

Soon afterwards he received a note from Mildred, informing him of their approaching return, and asking him to come and see her at luncheon, or any other time, during the course of the week. He did not wish to appear churlish in not responding to the invitation, so one morning, a very few days after the receipt of Lady Devereux's note, he started on his sturdy cob in the direction of Staplemoor. On arriving there he was informed that Lord Devereux had not yet returned from cub-hunting, but that her ladyship would see him.

Lady Devereux was just sitting down to luncheon when George was announced. Several additional places were laid on the chance of anybody dropping in; but she was still sitting alone at the table when he was shown in. Though it happened to be fortuitous, it would have been a stratagem worthy of a more scheming feminine mind than hers was to arrange that their first meeting should take place under such thoroughly conventional circumstances, when the presence of the servants and questions such as "Hashed venison or roast chicken?" prevented the conversation from leaving the ordinary range of commonplace topics, thus taking off the rough edge of whatever awkwardness a first interview might easily have engendered.

On the big folding doors being thrown open to admit him, his first impression was: How handsome she has grown! This was the purely material, optical impression similar to a negative taken by a camera; the reflex action produced upon the mind by what the eye saw was totally wanting. He could not but notice, however, the many improvements that had accompanied the transition from maiden to matron. The outlines of her face and figure had softened; her complexion had grown richer in tint, and the natural gracefulness and repose of her manner seemed thoroughly in keeping with the dignity of her new station. Those dark, pensive eyes, with their expression of candour and fearlessness; that pure white brow with the wavy hair growing low upon the forehead, all these were familiar enough to George; but they evoked no other feeling within him than that produced by a dispassionate gaze at a lovely work of art. Somehow, all fond memory of days gone by had vanished in the fiery furnace of passion through which he had passed; and the weary, wistful expression of his eyes seldom left them.

Mildred rose to greet him and met him with a look of friendly cordiality and sympathy. They had not seen each other for so long, that a very natural curiosity arose in her to judge for herself how fate had dealt with him during this, to both of them, eventful space of time. One glance sufficed for her to realise the change that had come over him. The bright, cheerful look, denoting self-confidence, hopefulness and enjoyment of life had departed; though the weeks spent in a sick room might account for the shrunk, haggard expression of his face, the discouraged, almost dejected look, and the sadness of the smile that greeted her, were clearly not due to physical suffering alone. Her heart sank at the sight, and every vestige of reproachfulness or bitterness vanished to make room for a sentiment of unbounded sympathy and compassion.

He sat down opposite her, and the warmth and geniality of her manner soon made him forget the apprehension with which he had looked forward to this first interview. Inquiries as to his health served as an introduction to the conversation, which soon flowed along easily and naturally on safe neutral topics. She questioned him as to the last new phase of his life, and to the amount of interest and occupation it afforded him, and expressed her satisfaction at having him in her near neighbourhood, which would enable her to enliven his solitude with whatever social resources Staplemoor might offer.

By the time luncheon was at an end all shyness on either side had worn off, and an easy, conventional footing had been established between the two. No allusion was made to the past; and Mildred discreetly avoided any questions as to his life in Hungary, which might have been apt to lead on to dangerous ground. When George took his leave, he did so with the impression of having spent an hour or two very pleasantly, but otherwise nothing was altered, and his solitary evening was lighted up by no remembrance of the meeting that would have relieved the sombre cast of his meditations.

There is a singularly expressive word in the German language, the word *Sehnsucht,* which would best describe George Mansfield's frame of mind at that time—a sort of superlative of longing and desire combined; that craving for but one more look at the face, absent and yet ever present, which nothing can satisfy or dispel but the actual presence of the object beloved.

CHAPTER XVIII.

"Look in my face; my name is Might-Have-Been;
I am also called No-More, Too-Late, Farewell;
Unto thine ear I hold the Dead Sea shell
Cast up thy life's foam-fretted feet between."
                              DANTE ROSSETTI.

FAR different and deeper had been the impression
which their first interview had produced upon Mildred. That the vocation of the ministering angel is
innate in almost every woman is a trite truism. In
her it existed in a highly developed state, and feelings of tender compassion would have been roused
within her even had no other sentiment for George
remained lurking in her heart. Whatever his wrongs
might have been, they were forgiven; for had they
not been too manifestly expiated? Her duty, therefore, was clearly to hold out a friendly and helping
hand, instead of sitting in judgment over him. She
did not stop to consider whether such a course might
not be fraught with some danger to herself, nor
would such a consideration have deterred her; so she
set herself the task of devising some scheme by
which George could be brought back to a more nor-
mal frame of mind and a more natural mode of
existence than the life of seclusion and monastic re-
tirement that he had for the time being selected.

Though by no means overrating the very limited amount of influence she could still hope to exercise over him, she nevertheless felt confident that through her instrumentality alone could the cure be effected. She paused for a moment in her reflections. The thought that, after her return, Mrs. Jack Arthur might very likely be not only willing, but even anxious, to relieve her of the self-imposed duty of bringing back George Mansfield to society, flashed across her mind, and did but confirm her in her resolution.

Her surmise with regard to the latter was speedily justified by events. The fact that Captain Atherstone had some time back resigned his proud position in her surroundings, as well as her former friendly intimacy with George Mansfield, militated strongly in favour of her not letting so valuable an opportunity pass of "paying out" Lady Devereux for any real or imaginary offences.

A note was consequently despatched by her very few days after her arrival, reminding George of old days, expressing her joy at his return, together with a request to come and see her within the next two or three days. The note was delivered to George one evening when he was deep in his meditations. The sight of the familiar writing only intensified the expression of weariness upon his face, and a muttered exclamation, that sounded very much like "Why can't the woman leave one alone?" escaped him. He was not in the humour to appreciate Mrs. Jack's flippant style of conversation; and the vision of the bright hue of her curls, her society jargon, her side-glances, and all the rest, almost sickened him.

At that time no doubt was left him that his days as a soldier were over, never to return again; for, although he could use his hand for most ordinary purposes, there was a stiffness left in the wrist that incapacitated him for military service. His taste for reading, temporarily subdued during his intimacy with Countess Szent Imre, had now come to the fore again. Many books which he had bought upon Father Vincent's recommendation, and which had remained untouched on their shelf for many months, he now took up, originally, no doubt chiefly from association of ideas that connected them with the past, but soon also from the growing interest they roused in his mind, sickened and wearied as it was with the so-called pleasures of life.

One of these books, over which he would spend many hours, was Thomas of Celano's quaint old monastic tale of the life of St. Francis. The simple, child-like faith that breathed from every line of this series of legends—partly pathetic, partly almost verging upon the grotesque, but all of them replete with the spirit of the age of the Crusades, and having, so to speak, as a background, the vine-clad, purple range of mountains surrounding the quaint old city of Assisi in its unique picturesqueness, and, above it, the cloudless blue of an Italian sky, appealed to his imagination and had a strange fascination for him.

The many long, solitary evenings he had spent had taught him to think—an occupation not often or easily indulged in in a life of which every hour is mapped out beforehand for purposes of duty or pleasure. That the current of his thoughts had been led into a channel towards which they certainly had never previously tended was undoubtedly, to a great extent, due to the influence of Father Vincent.

At first George had felt little more than curiosity concerning him, looking upon a man born and bred a gentleman, who led a life of absolute self-abnegation, poverty and lowliness, merely as a specimen of morbid religious fanaticism little short of monomania. It was only when he perceived what a wealth of knowledge, not only acquired by poring over volumes of paper and parchment, was buried under this humble surface; when he realised that this poor Franciscan monk was looked up to for miles around as the Father of the poor and the distressed, and that, so far from being, as he had anticipated, little short of a harmless lunatic, he was endowed with a clear and singularly penetrating gift of perception and judgment, that he had felt himself attracted towards him. Perhaps what impressed him more than anything else was the priest's look of serene, placid happiness, as if the cares of the world existed not for him, and as if in his eyes toil meant pleasure.

They had seen less of each other once George had given himself up, with all his heart and soul and strength, to his love for Countess Szent Imre; but during all the weeks that succeeded his accident, the monk hardly left his bedside; and, at the time of their parting, George could not but say to himself that he hardly had a better friend in the world than Father Vincent.

With her intimate knowledge of him, and the truly feminine tact which she possessed to a remarkable extent, Mildred had not been long in discovering the exact nature of the changes that his absence abroad had wrought in George's nature. She saw at a glance that the lighthearted man of pleasure existed no more, and that his character had gained in depth and earnestness. Far from regretting these changes, she saw in them only so many additional points of contact between all her innermost soul and that of her lost lover; and the only bitter pang she felt was that it had not been granted to her to be the means of effecting this change. All that in former days had acted rather as a check upon her feelings towards him: the apparently rather superficial view he would take of things; his worldliness and desire for pleasure and excitement, had vanished; and all that was noble and good in his nature had taken deeper root. She never questioned that had Fate ordained that their paths through life should be thrown together, the same result would have been achieved by her without his bearing that heavy burden of oppression and weariness.

All the shyness and restraint that had marked George's manner to her during their first interview had gradually worn off. Somehow, she appeared to him under a different light from what she did before. Not that she had altered in any way; only he was then far better able to appreciate many sides

in her nature which formerly were but a sealed book
to him. With the utmost frankness he told her how
heavily his obligation towards Lord Devereux weighed
upon him, and how firmly resolved he was gradually
to liberate himself from it; though he little guessed
that this transaction had been the cause of Mildred's
acting upon his advice, and accepting Lord Devereux's
proposal.

The new line his thoughts had taken created
many topics of mutual understanding between the
two, and Mildred sometimes inwardly smiled when
she looked back upon the days when she had read
and re-read with the utmost attention the sporting
column of the daily papers, in order not to show her
utter ignorance of one of her lover's favourite pursuits. In all her numerous errands of charity that
frequently took her to different parts of the estate,
Lady Devereux found in George a most willing and
useful companion, not only able to carry out her
wishes, but full of suggestions of his own, and of
keen interest in her work.

*   *   *   *   *

Christmas was drawing near when they started
out one morning together in Mildred's pony-cart for a
village situated some six or seven miles from Staplemoor. Lord Devereux troubled himself but little
about these excursions of his wife; he fully approved
of their purpose, which indirectly tended to increase
his own popularity in the country; but beyond that
he seldom questioned her as to her movements.
Whenever he met George Mansfield it was with the

utmost cordiality, and the thought that any harm might arise from his wife being frequently thrown together with her lover of old days never even crossed his mind.

Mildred's visit on that particular excursion was destined to the wife of a poor cottager outside the village of Brentham. The poor woman was only just recovered from her confinement, and the distress was increased by the fact of her husband—who, when not incapacitated by drink, would go and work at a neighbouring forge—being temporarily out of employment. After some inquiries, Lady Devereux and her escort found the cottage. The handle of the bell was broken, but a knock at the front door was soon answered by a wizened, pale-faced little girl, who stared in amazement at the stately figure descending from the pony-cart. The child blushed crimson, and dropping Mildred a curtsey, stammered out, in answer to an inquiry as to her mother's health: "Beg your pardon, milady, mother's very poorly indeed; the baby keeps a fretting of her all night, so mother don't get no sleep at all."

Mildred's manner towards the poor was the outcome of her natural kind-heartedness and genuine love of her suffering fellow-creatures. She was never at a loss as to what to say to them, and her manner was very different from that only too common when "slumming" in the East-end of London came into fashion. An apparition in gorgeous attire, evidently extremely ill at her ease, and cracking her head what to say, inwardly hoping there might be no infection about, and much pre-occupied by this consideration; a few stereotyped questions as to number and age of children; the hope expressed of speedy recovery, together with a vague promise of coming again; finally, half-a-sovereign left on the table, and a rapid exit, are scarcely the characteristics of a visit from which much lasting good can be expected.

The hamper containing Mildred's many little gifts in the shape of baby linen, beef-tea and similar most acceptable provisions having been duly unloaded, George drove the pony round to the adjacent inn, with instructions to join her again at the cottage. The sight that met Mildred's eye on entering the cottage was one that might have struck pity into a heart less impressionable than hers was. In a narrow iron bedstead, covered only with a blanket—the sheets had gone to the pawnbroker's long ago—lay the emaciated figure of a woman, who, until care and privation had done their handiwork, must have been by no means devoid of good looks. The pale, hollow cheeks made the deep blue eyes seem unnaturally large, and the fair hair that grew low upon the brow was streaked with grey in many places, though the woman could hardly be more than thirty. The thin, transparent hand hung listlessly over the bedside, intensifying the pathetic look of mute despair caused by years of suffering, mental and physical, and the knowledge that the return of health meant little more than the relief of a slight part of life's burden. The large eyes were turned anxiously, with the look of a hunted deer, towards the door as

Mildred entered. What ever crossed the poor friend-less woman's threshold but care, in some shape or other? Her husband reeling home from the public-house; an errand boy to say the baker could not give another loaf until he had received something on account; before long, very likely the bailiff to seize whatever scanty scraps of furniture were left.

A sigh of relief came from the poor invalid as, instead of any of the dreaded visions, she saw Lady Devereux coming in, gently and noiselessly, with a sweet smile on her lips and the light of sympathy and kindness upon her face. Mildred was too well known in the neighbourhood not to be recognised at the first glance, and, to the poor sufferer, she appeared almost as an angel of light and charity. She sat down by the bedside and, taking up the poor feverish hand, inquired with earnest sympathy into all the woman's troubles.

The tale was by no means an uncommon one. The daughter of well-to-do people, she had married against her parents' wish, and, after having seen better days, she had rapidly gone down hill. Her husband had taken to drink, and they had been obliged to shut up the little business they had started. With a rapidly increasing family and absolute misery staring her in the face, exposed to her husband's ruffianly brutality, her life had grown a burden al-most too heavy to bear.

The tears glistened in Mildred's eyes as she listened to this tale, pathetic in its simplicity and un-mistakable truthfulness. Very few questions sufficed to show her that the poor woman was above all in want of proper medical assistance; and, as soon as George had returned, she sent him off at once in search of the village doctor. The latter having fortunately been found at home, he proceeded at once, together with George, to where his services were required. Much remained for Mildred to do even after the doctor's visit. She suggested to George his returning to Staplemoor and sending back another carriage for her. This, however, he firmly declined to do; the day was sinking, and he had no intention of leaving her under the circumstances; so he settled himself down in the little apology for a parlour that adjoined the room in which the sick woman lay, alone with his thoughts.

Before very long the train of the latter was interrupted by a heavy footstep outside, and the door was opened with a savage wrench to admit the bulky form of the tenant of the cottage. Jim Styles—this was the man's name—was admitted, even by his friends, to be "a bit of an awkward customer when he had had a glass, though not a bad chap, take him all round." That he had, on the present occasion, "had a glass," or probably a good many, was palpable even to a less practised eye than George's (soldiering is apt to sharpen the eye to a considerable extent in the detection of this infirmity), though he had not yet reached the stage of reeling helplessness. His glassy eye fixed with a decidedly nasty expression upon the unexpected intruder, and before George had time to explain his presence, he found himself rather gruffly accosted in a loud and somewhat quarrelsome tone: "Well, and who might you be, if I may enquire? You seem to have made yourself quite at home in the place, anyhow."

George's prominent idea, under the circumstances, was to avoid anything in the shape of a quarrel on account of the poor woman, separated only by a thin door from the scene of the conversation. He therefore replied in the very meekest tone that he had accompanied Lady Devereux, who had come to see if she could offer any assistance to the invalid in the next room. The answer was both in tone and meaning so eminently conciliatory that quarrelsome as the blacksmith's mood was, he could not very well pretend to take offence at it; so he merely shrugged his shoulders, muttering between his lips something about fine folks minding their own business. At the same time he made a move towards the door that led into the room where Mildred was sitting by the bedside of the sick woman. Seeing the state he was in and guessing what effect his exceedingly ill-timed intrusion would have upon both the inmates of the room, George mildly interposed, remarking that the doctor had recommended the most absolute quiet as an indispensable condition for the recovery of the invalid, at the same time suggesting that the other should return in an hour's time, when Lady Devereux would be leaving and the patient would very likely have fallen asleep.

Excellent though his intentions no doubt were, his interposition, under the circumstances, was

scarcely judicious, for it suited the other's purpose
of picking a quarrel; all the more so as George had
risen and placed himself in a quiet but resolute attitude in front of the door. No more was required
to rouse every savage instinct within the blacksmith,
whose blood was heated by copious libations that increased tenfold the natural combativeness of the man.
Abandoning the slouching attitude which intemperance had given him, he raised himself to his full
height, and throwing back his powerful shoulders, he
said, adorning his words with many vigorous and
vicious expletives: "And so you think you are going
to order me about in my own house, do you? Well,
all I can say you'll find yourself out of your reckon-
ing at that game. Perhaps you don't know Jim
Styles, and you'll think better of it when you do.
Stand aside there, you!"

George never moved an inch. When the other's
voice dropped for a moment, he could faintly discern
in the next room the plaintive, pitiful notes of the
poor sick woman and Mildred's words of comfort
and encouragement. He felt himself in a thoroughly
awkward position: if he admitted the man into the
room, blind with drink and frenzy as he was, it was
hard to tell upon whom his fury and his foul language would vent itself. Absolutely fearless as far
as he was concerned, he once more tried his powers
of persuasion, endeavouring to explain what his
motives were and recommending his adversary to return in an hour's time, when, if sober, he should find
the passage unimpeded. Surely he must be able to

understand that Lady Devereux had come merely
from kindness towards his wife. These arguments
proved of no avail, for the blacksmith did not mean
to be done out of the fight he was longing for by
any amount of persuasion.

"That's all mighty fine," was the retort, "but if
her ladyship wanted to see my wife, what business
have you here? When fine ladies come and see us
poor folk, let them leave their sweethearts at home."

Before another word had escaped his lips George
interrupted him. He had turned as white as a sheet,
and his mouth was twitching with suppressed emotion: "Look here, my good man, this sort of thing
won't do; you'll either keep a civil tongue in your
head or you will take the consequences."

"Consequences be d——d!" said the other, at
the same time leading off with a heavy blow straight
at George's face. The latter had too much experience to have taken his eye off that of his op-
ponent for a moment, though he was determined to
avoid opening hostilities. Thus he was not taken
unawares, and ducked, thereby escaping a formidable
left-hander. At the same time he countered heavily
and landed his left on to his adversary's jaw. The
blow was a powerful one; George's blood was up,
and he put, perhaps, rather more "body" into it than
the circumstances absolutely demanded. Anyhow,
with a loud crash, that knocked over a table and
demolished the scant amount of crockery the cottage
could boast of, the blacksmith fell to the ground.

There was nothing in his fall to cause any immediate anxiety; so, before troubling himself about him, George quickly entered the bedroom where Mildred and the poor sick woman were. The look of anguish on the latter's face went straight to his heart, and he hastened to reassure her, explaining matters as best he could. He then told Mildred in very few words how the thing had happened, and then returned to see how his late adversary was doing. Still on the floor, though only in a half-recumbent position, the blacksmith was rubbing his head, which, in his fall, had come into collision with some piece of furniture. There was a dazed expression about his face, and he was looking around him with a stare as if endeavouring to collect his thoughts.

All combativeness had left him, and his former defiant tone was changed into one of plaintive humility. He was beside himself, he said; privation and the sickness of his wife had upset him altogether. George was overjoyed that so little damage had been done; he inquired into the man's antecedents and endeavoured to offer whatever comfort he could.

Whilst he was thus talking, Mildred came into the room. Her beauty, added to the calm dignity of her manner, would probably have disarmed the man who now sat there, the picture of abject misery, even in his most savage mood. He felt so thoroughly ashamed of himself that he scarcely dared raise his eyes from the ground, and avoided the gaze of those deep blue eyes that looked at him so earnestly and compassionately.

"I think your wife is a little better now," she said. "The doctor has prescribed for her; but he says himself that all his prescriptions will do her no good without rest and kind treatment. Surely you would not wish to make her more miserable than she already is; I cannot believe you to be so unmanly. I mean to come and see her again in two or three days; only, if you are once more as you were to-day, Lord Devereux would not allow me to come. Can I trust you? Would it be so very hard to turn over a new leaf?" She held out her hand to the man as she spoke. There was nothing of the ruffian as he is seen on the stage in poor Jim Styles, or he would have bathed the proffered hand with tears and not unlikely have kissed the hem of her skirt. Nothing of the kind entered his mind; but with a vigorous grasp of the hand he only said, in a voice that was husky, not solely from recent intemperance:

"I know you are right, milady, in all you say; and I've been a shocking bad husband to poor Lottie, and it's been a poor return for all she has done for me; but I'll try and do as you say, for the sake of you that has asked me to do it; and if I don't keep my promise my name ain't Jim Styles. And now shall I run and get your ladyship's trap round?"

This offer Mildred declined, and so she and George left together to fetch the pony-cart from the neighbouring inn, which was only some two or three minutes' walk from there. Darkness was beginning to set in when they started off for their long drive home.

For some time they sat silently next to each other. At last George began:

"I should not be at all surprised if that man were to keep his promise and lead a more decent life in future. I wonder what occult charm you have that gives you the power you have over all men, even when they are made of such tough fibre as our friend the blacksmith?"

"Nonsense, my dear George! I have no power over anybody; I often wish I had. That poor man was so dazed after your rough treatment that he would have promised anything to anybody. I fancy it was more your fists than my eloquence that made what you call the tough fibre rather more supple. I only hope he may remember his promise when he is quite sober again."

They were each of them following out the train of their reflections, and another long silence ensued.

"How ungrateful it does seem of all of us," at last said Mildred, "always being discontented and fretful—inwardly, anyhow, even if we don't show it to our surroundings—when we compare our life to that of that poor woman. Now what has life been to her but privation, disappointment, humiliation? I suppose she cared for this man, or she could not have married him; and see how he treats her! Yet

she makes much less fuss about herself than I often
do about my more or less imaginary woes."

"But what are these woes, imaginary or otherwise?" he replied, with perfectly unassumed ignorance.

"Oh, nothing particular," she answered.

The words that had been uttered barely an hour
ago by that drunken ruffian rankled in George's mind.
True, the source from which they came made them
almost beneath contempt; and yet, what this man
had said might only have been repeated from what
he had heard from others; and the mere notion of
any breath of slander attaching itself to Mildred's
fair name was in itself intolerable to him. Once
already he had wronged her, early in life, no doubt
owing to no immediate fault of his. Was he now
deliberately, and with his eyes open, to inflict further
injury upon her? The current of his thoughts brought
him back to old times.

"My remark is a commonplace one," he said,
"I warn you beforehand, but the truth of the old
saying that a life's destiny may depend upon the
veriest trifle was brought home to me rather more
forcibly than usual. What could have been more of
a chance than you hearing about this poor woman,
or your going to see her? And now, if only that
drunken husband of hers, whom you have bewitched,
will be true to his word, it may be the turning point
in her existence. And again, in our own lives: you
remember the day of the Hunt Cup? Suppose little
Davis, who was riding Barrister, had for a moment
lost his own head and let go of his horse's when it

came to the pinch—he had done it many a time before, and I suppose he has since—the *coup* would have been landed, and——"

"And——?"

"Well, I suppose we should have been happy ever after, like people in the fairy tale. Anyhow, it's a comfort to think that I have been the only loser by it."

There was no tone of bitterness in the remark; but it stung Mildred nevertheless.

"And yet, if I am well informed, you did not spend *all* your time weeping over Paradise Lost whilst you were out in Hungary."

"No; especially not after I heard of your engagement."

It cost Mildred a violent effort to restrain herself from telling him the whole truth there and then; but her lips remained sealed.

"Don't let us spoil what has, after all, been a very successful day by harping on things that belong to a distant past; they will never be wiped out from my memory"—she laid some stress on the *"my"*— "but no good can come from referring to them. Perhaps all is for the best as it is. When are you going back to Hungary to take leave of your regiment —soon, I suppose?"

"I was thinking of going out next week, but it makes but little difference to anybody whether I go sooner or later."

"I wish you would not talk in that desponding way, as if there was nothing left in life to interest you. Surely, if you are bored with the monotony of country life, and your farm is not enough to occupy your mind, you might create for yourself other subjects of interest. Your life would no longer be a blank, and you would not look so unhappy. Will you try? It makes me quite sad to see you in your present state."

"I will do my best," George replied laughingly, "to be less of a wet blanket in future, if only to please you; but you must allow I have been rather unlucky, having to leave just as I was beginning to get on nicely. However, I dare say I shall be all right again—my spirits, I mean—before very long."

Their conversation was brought to a close as they were driving up to the porticoed front door of Staplemoor; and they parted with the mutual agreement that the adventures of the day should remain strictly between themselves.

Mildred felt tired and rather weary on returning home, and she was rather glad to hear that Lord Devereux was dining out at a bachelors' party; so she would have the evening alone with her friend Mrs. Garrard, who was the only guest at the time. They were in Mildred's boudoir after dinner, dressed in tea-gowns, seated in comfortable arm-chairs, each of them with a book in her hand, though apparently not much disposed to do more than glance listlessly over the pages.

"How tired you look, Mildred," Mrs. Garrard began. "You have made rather too long a day of it; I should give anything to know what you and

Lord George could have found to talk about during all those many hours you spent together. Don't you think people will find it rather odd, supposing they met you? For, after all, nobody will believe that if you take a big Guardsman with you when you go and see a poor woman after her confinement it is only for *her* benefit, will they?"

"What nonsense you do talk!" Lady Devereux replied laughingly. "Of course he never even saw her, or, at least, he was not meant to see her. No, if I take him with me, it is for his sake, just to break the chain of his broodings; all those numberless hours he spends alone are so bad for him."

"You are quite sure it is not partly for your own sake that you see so much of him, are you?" Mildred coloured visibly; but the other went on in her brisk, cheery manner: "And does he tell you about the subject of his broodings, and are you expected to console him? Mind you, I always did like Lord George, and I do now; but I don't want you to get talked about because of your endeavour to dispel the blue devils from out of him. Mrs. Jack Arthur would tell you it is not worth while getting talked about for nothing at all. However, that is not the line of argument I mean to take with a high-minded person like you." She had drawn nearer to her friend and was leaning over the back of her chair, her face nearly touching that of Mildred. "I don't want to play the part of the croaking Cassandra, but, believe me, dear child, you live too much up in the clouds; I know men better than you do. Of course we know Lord George has had some sort of romance out there, and has not yet got over it, more's the luck. The day he does, beware!" Her voice had dropped almost to a whisper. "I can see you care for him as much as you ever did. Don't tell me you don't. I can see it in a hundred little things. Now, don't be angry with me."

Mildred sat perfectly immovable, never taking her eyes from the fire, as if intently watching the little blue flames that shot up now and then from between the embers.

"Of course I am not angry with you, Maggie, how could I be? But don't worry yourself about me; it is all quite different from what you fancy; and even if I did still like him it would make but little difference, for he loves another woman with all his heart and soul. Of course he has not told me so, but a child could see it. In fact, I believe he is going back to see her next week. It makes me miserable seeing him so dull and depressed, that's all. As to people talking, they will have to talk pretty loudly before it affects his lordship; and if they did most of his friends would only like me the better, and would find me far more congenial than they do at present. Do you suppose I care if Mrs. Jack Arthur abuses me a little more or less? Not I!"

CHAPTER XIX.

"I have had joy and sorrow; I have proved
What life could give; have loved and been beloved."
    *   *   *   *   *   *

"I am sick and heartsore
And weary, let me sleep;
But deep, deep,
Never to wake more."
MRS. JAMESON.

TEN days later George Mansfield was once more back in Hungary to take leave of his regiment.

The genuine ring of all the words of regret which he heard from his Colonel and his brother officers went straight to his heart. He had grown a general favourite with them all, and his voice shook with emotion when, at a farewell dinner, he got up to thank them for all the expressions of good feeling that had been used about himself. He could truthfully say that he would look back upon the time he had spent with them as one of the happiest periods of his life.

On the following day he drove over to Erdelyi to take leave of his troop. On re-entering the little village and driving up before the humble cottage so inseparably connected in his mind with all the joys and sorrows of the past, he could hardly bring

himself to realise that this was really his final farewell. It seemed to him like returning to his own
home, and the friendly look of welcome with which
even the peasants greeted him as his carriage rolled
past made him look upon them as something more
than mere supernumeraries in a scene where he had
met with nothing but hearty goodwill and kindness.
In the afternoon the troop paraded before him for
the last time, just outside the village. A look of
heartfelt regret and sadness came over the honest,
stolid countenances of these rough fellows when
George, addressing them in their own language, informed them that, owing to circumstances over
which he had no control, he was obliged to take
leave of the regiment; that no one could regret it
more deeply than he did, as it would have been his
pride and his ambition to lead into action a troop of
cavalry so thoroughly efficient as they were. Though,
of course, military etiquette forbade any response on
the part of the men thus addressed, they made up
for it later in the day, and, at an out-of-door enter-
tainment which George provided for them in the
afternoon, his health was drunk over and over again,
the men lifting their *pan porucznik* (officer) upon
their shoulders in the true old polish fashion.

On inquiring after his friend and companion
during the weary weeks of his illness, George was
informed that Father Vincent had suddenly been
summoned to Rome, and it was doubtful when he
would return. The news came upon him as a real
disappointment; for the link that connected these

natures, originally as distant from each other as the poles, had not been severed by George's departure, and at regular intervals a not infrequent correspondence had keen kept up between the two.

He had received a note from Countess Szent Imre asking him to come over in the afternoon and stay for dinner, if he was able to face a very dull party; for, not knowing the exact date of his return, she had asked some very uninteresting country neighbours; but they would be able to have a quiet talk the next morning if he wished. George had for some weeks back prepared himself and braced up his nerves for this final interview. He had repeated to himself, many and many a time, that it was nothing more than a formal farewell visit to a very dear friend, and he felt firmly resolved to avoid any sort of reference to the past. Presumably he really intended rigorously to carry out this programme, and felt confident in his ability to do so, blind to the fact that less than a glance—merely the raising of those drooping eyelids with their curly fringe by the tenth part of an inch, was required to upset the fabric of his resolutions.

Dense black clouds had risen on the horizon early in the day and, driven along by an easterly wind that blew in great gusts, they had rapidly spread and were beginning to discharge thick, heavy snow-flakes that soon began to lie on the hard-frozen, slippery roads. As George drove cautiously over the little wooden bridge just outside the village, and the long vista of the avenue of poplars that extended to the park gates of Kisfalva opened up once more before his eyes, his thoughts wandered back to a lovely moonlit summer night when he had driven home over that same bridge, his heart overflowing with exultant joy, when he saw opening up before him a cloudless horizon of love and blissful happiness; and he could not help wondering whether at the bottom of that now frozen brook the ring still lay which, on that night, he had thrown away as a pledge to Fate that the last link between himself and his former love was severed.

Every landmark along that bleak avenue, swept by fierce gusts of snow and sleet, was familiar to his eye and seemed to greet him like an old friend returned after a long absence; and as he drove past the lodge and over the drawbridge that led into the court, George felt his heart beating, however much he might try to persuade himself that he was only paying a commonplace visit of farewell.

The rules of Hungarian etiquette do not impose upon the large array of retainers that form part of every establishment the same stolid, dispassionate expression and gaze which our servants seem to have so little difficulty in acquiring, as if the joys and troubles of their masters and their masters' friends affected them no more than the vicissitudes of the inhabitants of some other planet. The pleasant, genial manner which George always adopted towards his inferiors had made him exceedingly popular amongst the vast retinue of the Kisfalva establishment; and the expressions of respectful welcome, coupled with the hope that he would not have to leave again, were plentiful. The bad state of the road had delayed his arrival beyond the time he had anticipated; nevertheless he was informed that none of the other guests had arrived, and that he would find the Countess in the library. The latter was a long, narrow gallery rather than a room; the lofty walls were covered throughout with bookcases containing many valuable volumes, though of a comparatively recent date; for the original family library had been destroyed in one of the many invasions of the Turks. The deep recesses formed by the windows in the walls of about six feet in thickness, contained writing-tables, couches and a few arm-chairs, chosen more with a view to the comfort of the exhausted student than from any artistic merit. Huge logs had been piled upon the grate of the monumental fireplace, a masterpiece of carved oak, and the fitful light from the fire was scarcely sufficient to remove the impression of semi-obscurity upon entering the library.

Not far from the fireplace, in one of the further recesses, a reading-lamp was burning, casting the warm tints of its shaded rays upon Countess Szent Imre's delicate features. She was writing busily, and not until George stood close to the table did she raise her eyes, without interrupting her writing: "That is not really you, is it? I cannot believe it. I know this sounds inhospitable, after writing to invite you, but you know what I mean. You must not mind my just finishing this letter, post goes in two minutes and I dare not miss it. Go and get warm by the fire, or else look at some of these old books; I shall not be half a minute."

George did not avail himself of the permission to take down any of the grim, vellum-bound volumes that frowned upon him as if only too conscious that he had not come on their account. Noiselessly, so as not to disturb her, he sat down on the side of an arm-chair, and took a long, loving look at that serene and placid countenance. The light was falling full upon her face, bringing out in clear relief, like a cameo, the delicate lineaments of her profile against the sombre hue of the curtain beyond. The innate gracefulness that stamped all her movements and attitudes was never more clearly perceptible. She sat perfectly erect, the delicate fingers of her left hand resting lightly upon the paper over which the quill pen was skimming at a rapid pace, the boldness of her firm and rather upright characters dispensing her from bringing her eyes into close proximity with the paper.

After a few minutes she closed her letter with a sigh of relief. "Maintenant je suis à vous," she said. "And now you are to tell me all about yourself—mind you, *all*, ever since the day I saw you last."

George thereupon began to describe his life during the past months, his various pursuits, and how he had been trying to take some sort of interest in his new occupations, etc. His account omitted nothing, except the large part she still played in his existence: for of this he breathed not a word. She listened intently; "And how about Lady Devereux? I hope I am not treading on delicate ground; do you often meet her? She is a near neighbour of yours now, isn't she?"

"Yes, I see her pretty often."

"Have you ever spoken to her about me?"

"Your name has hardly ever been mentioned between us."

The Countess was determined to keep the conversation on safe neutral ground during this first interview, so she rattled away lightly, telling him all the trifling news of the neighbourhood—discussing various changes that had occurred in the regiment since his absence; informing him who the guests were, whom she expected to dinner, etc. Thus the half-hour before dressing time was passed entirely in conformity with Countess Szent Imre's wishes, as well as with those which George had been endeavouring to inculcate upon himself.

And yet, needless to say, before he had been in her presence but a few minutes all his resolutions had faded away, and a wild, passionate longing to press those tempting lips but once more against his own caused all his blood to course feverishly through his veins. He sought his room thoroughly discontented with the Countess, with himself and the world in general. The effects of the mental discipline he had been undergoing during the last few months had vanished for the moment, swept away by an angry tumult of passion, though it would have been dif-

ficult for him to put the exact nature of his grievance
into words.

The company assembled for dinner when George
came down was larger than he anticipated; for
hitherto, owing to the Count's failing health, the
doors of the old castle of Kisfalva had been closed
against all but a very few intimate friends. It seemed
almost strange to him at last to see something of the
Countess' existence, of which, up to then, he knew
nothing; and he could not help noticing the gracefulness and distinction with which she did the
honours of her house; talking with the same listless
affability to a country curate pouring forth the woes
of his flock as she did to the handsome and cynical
Hungarian magnate sitting by her side, as he related
to her some highly flavoured anecdote that he had
picked up in the gilded salons of Monte Carlo.
George was told off to the daughter of a neighbouring landowner, whom he had met once or twice before. It did not matter much to him whom he took
in, so long as no great conversational efforts were
required of him. Whatever his own views might be,
his neighbour had no intention of spending a dull
evening, or allowing herself to be bored by him or
anybody else.

Jet-black hair, and eyes as big as tea-cups, that
smiled even during the rare intervals when her lips
did not; teeth of almost unnatural whiteness, that
made people forget the mouth, which was scarcely as
small as perfect symmetry would have exacted—
these were the most striking points in Etelka Mol-

nary's outward appearance. She thoroughly enjoyed life, of the intricacies of which she no doubt pretended to know far more than she really could know at the age of nineteen. Untroubled by any constitutional shyness, she gave free vent to her natural talkativeness. Thus time passed quickly enough for George, who, like most men in his frame of mind, betook himself somewhat assiduously to drowning care with some of the excellent vintage which the Kisfalva cellars still held.

"How handsome the Countess is looking to-night," his neighbour said to him rather abruptly, following the direction of his eyes. "I have not seen her in a low frock for ever so long. And how well she carries off all those heavy rows of pearls."

This remark gave George an excuse for allowing his eyes to wander with more persistence towards his lovely hostess. She was in black: a dress of great simplicity, but for that very reason best suited to enhance the beauty of the delicate outline of her figure, and setting off the snowy whiteness of the statuesque neck and shoulders. In her hair she wore as only ornament a crescent of brilliants, which stood off in bold relief from the thick auburn curls. The listlessness of her manner had apparently disappeared for the time being, and she seemed absorbed in conversation with her left-hand neighbour —an elderly man, with a greyish beard and spectacles.

"Who is that the Countess is talking to with so

much animation?" George asked his neighbour. "Somehow, I don't think I have ever seen his face before; can you tell me?"

"Oh! don't you know? That is one of the members of the Cabinet; they say he is shortly going to resign on account of his health, and there is some question of Count Kesthelyi's being his successor. You have heard of *him* surely, haven't you? I believe he used to be very devoted to the Countess some years ago; at least, so they say."

No need, indeed, to ask George if that name was familiar to him? Had he forgotten it? The altered expression, the unwonted animation brought about by the mere thought of her former lover, and the manner in which she listened with silent attention to the replies which her neighbour gave her in grave and measured tones would have sufficiently indicated to him the subject of their conversation. However, he was determined that nothing in his manner should betray his preoccupation, either to his neighbour or to his lovely hostess sitting opposite; so he responded with some alacrity to the lively remarks of the pretty girl next to him, though straining his ears now and then to catch a passing remark of the conversation on the other side of the table.

When dessert was being handed round, Mademoiselle Molnary turned towards George and said laughingly: "Well, I suppose all's well that ends well. I hope you have not been too dreadfully bored, but if you have I will allow you have borne it like a man. Do you suppose I don't know where your thoughts were the whole time? Anyhow, your penance is nearly over now, for of course you know we all go out together."

George responded with the compliment, obvious under the circumstances; and very shortly afterwards the signal of departure for the drawing-room was given.

In Hungary, as in many Continental countries, cigarettes and cigars form a *sine qua non* of post-prandial conversation; and the ladies not joining in the after-dinner smoke form an almost imperceptible minority. The association between smoking and manners, either fast, loud or otherwise unconventional, so prevalent with us, is totally unknown in Hungary, where it is the rule, and not the exception, and where exemplary matrons, mothers of families, whose worst enemies would not suspect them of being fast, can be seen nightly enjoying their weed of five or six inches long.

After half-an-hour's interval, devoted to rather listless general talk, a stir was noticeable, and the usual entreaty of "Do sing something!" was ad-dressed to the Countess in the proper imploring tone. She had fully anticipated this request, and expressed her willingness to accede to it. For a few moments her taper fingers, with the highly-polished nails, wandered about listlessly over the keys; but her in-decision was never of long duration, and, with a rapid glance in the direction of where George was sitting, she struck up, in her lovely contralto voice, the opening bars of one of Grieg's softest melodies.

When the echo of the last strains had died away, she rose, and no amount of entreaty prevailed upon her to sing another note. By an almost imperceptible raising of the eyebrows, she signified to George her wish to speak to him; and, without attracting anybody's attention, they soon found themselves together in the boudoir adjoining the drawing-room.

"Did you recognise that song you have just heard?" said the Countess, with her sweetest smile. "I sang it on purpose to please you; I thought it might remind you of something."

"So it did; it reminded me, to use a very hackneyed quotation from Dante: 'Nessun maggior dolore,' etc.

The terrible earnestness of his tone was in striking contrast with the perfectly placid look upon her face, and the rather *distrait* manner in which she occasionally glanced towards the heavy portières that separated them from the other room.

"Don't be afraid," he added; "I shall not detain you many minutes, and your guests seem perfectly happy listening to Mademoiselle Molnary; and surely you must have had plenty of time all through dinner to acquire all the information you wanted from that old Cabinet Minister. It was satisfactory, I hope? Do you remember telling me, not so very long ago, that for you the past was buried, and that the requiescat on the grave of your first love could never be moved? Are you sure the epitaph ought not to be 'Resurgam'?"

"Perhaps you are right," she answered, in a low tone, as if speaking to herself. And, after a short pause, she added: "I never was deceitful, whatever my other faults may have been. I look upon you as the soul of loyalty and honour, and I owe you the whole truth. Will you for a moment carry your thoughts back to some six months ago? I told you from the first not to care for me, and that I had nothing to give you in return. I laid out before you my whole life's history to read like an open book, and withheld nothing. Of course I was weak—sadly weak with you; but, if I was, it is scarcely for you to reproach me with it, is it? You must allow that never for a moment did I lead you to suppose you could take the part in my life that he did. By some strange fatality you were thrown across my path at a very critical moment in my life. What I had suffered no one—not even you—can ever realise. I had no one in whom I could confide— no one to whom to look for sympathy. Then I met you. From the very first you seemed to understand me: I felt I could trust you. I never meant you to be more to me than a true and trusting friend. I did not wish you to care for me as you did. My pride suffered intensely—you know through what; and I saw how devotedly fond you had grown of me. What more need I say? Soon after you left, by the greatest chance I met once more the man who has been the evil genius of my life. He begged hard to be forgiven; he swore he had never loved any other woman than me. And shall I tell you the whole truth? I felt lowered—dreadfully lowered—in my own eyes, when I thought of you and all these past months. I had once dreamt that I might be different from other women, that I might have kept myself wholly for the one great love of my life. I should have done so had it not been for you; and, believe me, I have passed through many moments of late when I hated and despised myself. Of course, I grant that you have some cause to say or think all sorts of unkind and ill-natured things about me. If you are able to understand a woman's nature—or, at least, if you can understand mine—I don't think you will. Now, don't be too unhappy. I have told you the whole truth; and now I must go and see what those people are doing in there." And, holding out her little hand for him to kiss, she rose to leave the room.

"Don't go just yet," was all he could find to say. "You forget that these few moments may decide my whole future life."

With a look of weariness and compassion more than affection, she let herself drop once more into the arm-chair she had been occupying. "What is the good," she said in a low tone, "of going over and over again the same ground? I am a poor hand at making conventional speeches. Do you want me to say I will not forget you, or that I will write to you? Will that make you any happier?" Her tone softened as she added: "I don't want us to part in anger, still less do I wish to give you more pain than I can help. Believe me it is best as it is. I sometimes feel I have absorbed far too great a part of your thoughts, of your life, I may say. A woman's love is not enough to fill a man's life. There is much in you that could be devoted to a far nobler pursuit than trying to win me—or to win me back, I suppose I must say. Will you try for my sake? And at least I shall feel my influence over you has not been altogether a bad one, as your friend, Father Vincent, always endeavours to persuade me it has been. By-the-bye, he left this letter for you in case I were to see you on your return," and she rose to open her despatch-box.

Taking the letter, George pressed her hand devoutly to his lips and said: "Very well, be it as you say. It will always be my greatest pride to have won even the passing affection of the best and noblest of women I have ever met. Bless you. Good-bye!"

Two or three seconds later they listlessly strolled into the room where the assembled company was frantically applauding a duet that had just come to an end.

The next morning they parted, never to meet again on this side of the grave.

When George Mansfield returned to his room that evening there was a look on his face, not of despair or weariness, but rather of resignation and manly courage. He felt, not that a phase of his life was at an end, but that the curtain had dropped on all his past life. With feverish haste he opened the letter the Countess had given him from the Franciscan monk. It was headed

OSPEDALE DI SANTA MADDALENA, NAPLES.

DEAR LORD GEORGE,—I trust this may reach you. My life here is a busy one, so excuse the brevity of this letter.

Since the terrible outbreak of cholera six weeks ago that is decimating the population here I have been told off to this hospital. There is much work to be done; the people are panic-stricken, and from sheer terror fly into the very jaws of sickness and death. We are now having up to one thousand cases a day spread over every district of the town, and we can scarcely collect the hands to bury the dead. The staff of the hospital is reduced by sickness and overwork, and the strain upon the survivors is such that they cannot bear it long. If you have any opportunity of collecting funds do so, for they are sorely needed.

I trust you are well both in mind and body.

I am thankful to have been granted the opportunity of helping my suffering brethren.

FATHER VINCENT.

When George Mansfield reached the end of this letter every vestige of fretfulness or despondency disappeared from his countenance to give place to an expression of calm determination. He had said farewell to the world, its pomps and vanities; his path lay clear and open before him. Within a few minutes his decision was come to; what he longed for was work, which alone would give him oblivion. He sat up a great part of the night writing letters to his brother, to Mildred, to Father Vincent, announcing his arrival within a week, and finally to Countess Szent Imre. To her he wrote:—

When this reaches you I shall have left Kisfalva, never to see it again.

I can now say good-bye free from all bitterness and rancour. Taking leave of you means to me much more than you perhaps fancy. I know I was nothing but a passing episode in your life. I say this with no resentment. You did nothing to make me care for you, and no woman could have behaved more loyally or straightforwardly than you did from first to last.

I am leaving almost immediately for Naples. Father Vincent tells me there is much work to be done in the cholera hospital, and they are terribly short of hands. Do you remember once quoting to me the words, taken I don't know whence: "En fait d'hommes, je ne comprends que deux types: Don Juan ou Saint-François d'Assise?" I am no good in the capacity of the former, so I will, anyhow for a time, strive to follow to the best of my ability in the footsteps of the latter.

Bitterness as to the past, jealousy as to the future, seem to me now like words of a half-forgotten language.   May every happiness be yours.

G. M.

Every line you have ever written to me is burnt. Good-bye.

CHAPTER XX.

"The air of death breathes through our souls,
 The dead around us lie;
 By day or night, the death-bell tolls
 And says: 'Prepare to die.'"
JOHN WILSON.

IT is not very many years since the cholera scourge visited Naples in its full severity. From the lofty heights of the Castello down to where the promontory of Posilippo stretches out far into the deep blue surface of the Bay, there was scarcely a street that escaped the visit of the Angel of Destruction, carrying off indiscriminately young and old—men of lofty rank, round whose bedside learned professors sat in consultation, and the poor, half-starved lazzaroni who, like the troglodytes of old, lived in the damp grottoes of the Fondaci. As if in bitter mockery of the puerile precautions that human ingenuity could devise—the quarantines by land and sea, the fumigations, domiciliary visits, etc.—the Fiend took from week to week a firmer grip of the unfortunate city that lay prostrate at his feet, until from those shores, once resonant with the sounds of the mandoline and the joyous chorus of the *barcaiuoli*, a wail of anguish rose to heaven clamouring for mercy and deliverance. The ordinary hospital accommodation soon proved uttery inadequate; the wooden huts on the heights of the Campo di Marte used for barracks in ordinary times, were filled to overflowing, and yet there were no signs of the scourge relenting. Stimulated by the noble example of their King, the authorities did all in their power to stem the current; but the panic-stricken population paid little heed to the deliberations of the wise men sitting together in council.

When they felt the first symptoms of the *brutto morbo*—the word cholera was superstitiously banished —they would mutter a prayer to their guardian saints; and amongst the lower classes many would refuse to leave their underground dwellings, reeking with damp and the effluvia of the drains. A childish terror had seized their minds, for they feared that the arrival of medical assistance meant certain death; and in innumerable cases the physicians who came to administer relief were refused admittance and warned off the premises with sinister threats.

Nevertheless, and although struggling against almost insurmountable difficulties, the doctors stuck to their work manfully and courageously, even when their steadily diminishing number made the task of successfully grappling with the epidemic an almost hopeless one. The hospital nurses were dying off rapidly, partly from the disease itself, partly from overwork and sheer exhaustion; and even the men required to take the dead to their last resting-place were scarcely obtainable.

"Lei va a Napoli?" (You are going to Naples?)

said, in a surprised tone, the station-master at Rome to George, as the latter enquired when the next train was leaving. On being answered in the affirmative, the official blandly remarked that all trains but two per diem had been taken off. "For," he added with a smile, "there are not many people who want to go to Naples just now." However, George's patience was not put to a very severe test, and a few hours afterwards the train for Naples drew up alongside the platform, the officials looking with awe-struck curiosity at the handsome young *forestiere* going, as they considered, into the very jaws of death. "Dev' esser Inglese" (He must be an Englishman), said one to the other, slightly raising his eyebrows, as if this were a sufficient explanation of almost any form of eccentricity.

Before the train started, George noticed a closely-locked third-class carriage next to his, the sole occupant of which was a sinister-looking individual, reeking of chloral acid and other disinfectants. On enquiring after the purpose of this carriage, George was informed it was reserved for any passengers falling ill *en route,* who would then be entrusted to the care of the individual he had noticed. "May heaven preserve me from such a fate!" our friend muttered to himself; and settling himself to rest in his empty carriage, he was soon sound asleep.

The sun was shining brightly when he awoke from his slumbers. One glance sufficed to show him that he was approaching his destination; for at the foot of the steep embankment on which the train was slowly steaming along lay the Bay of Naples in its matchless glory, with the islands of Capri, Ischia and Procida rising out of the veil of purple mist that hung around them. A few minutes later the train drew up at a platform deserted save by a few *cara-binieri* strutting about in their cocked hats and closely scrutinising the only first-class passenger as he alighted from his carriage. There was none of the bustle and excitement common to most railway stations; a gloomy silence reigned everywhere, and the air was redolent of the acrid fumes of carbolic acid with which the vast building reeked.

Collecting his scanty belongings, George made his way to the exit and hailed the solitary cab within sight. Upon being asked "A che albergo" (To what hotel?), he replied: "All Ospedale de Santa Maddalena" (To the St. Magdalen hospital), at the same time depositing his bag next to the driver. The effect produced by these words was magical; for one second the man stared at him with the expression of terror clearly depicted in his face. He then flung the bag to the ground and, whipping up his horse, departed at a gallop. The incident was so unexpected that George burst out laughing, and was thankful, after much explanation, to find a porter who consented, upon the promise of ample remuneration, to carry his portmanteau as far as the gates of the hospital. Following in the man's footsteps the traveller threaded his way through the deserted streets.

In spite of the very early hour the church bells were ringing, calling the faithful to their matinal

devotions, and thither the few passers-by whom
George encountered were plainly directing their hurried footsteps—otherwise no sign of life was perceptible. But if the vast city, with its hundreds of
thousands of inhabitants densely packed together,
too many of them, in dwellings not worthy of human
beings, was endeavouring to find in its slumbers
oblivion of the horrors of the preceding day before
encountering those that were to follow, the Angel of
Death took no rest and respected neither time nor
circumstance.

Turning into one of the main thoroughfares, a
ghastly procession met George's eye. The impressive
solemnity of the funeral rites—the hearse bedecked
with wreaths and evergreens, followed by priests
chanting the sacred strains of the *Dies iræ*, the
mourning coaches and all the other tributes of respect
and of loving memory to the dead had long been
done away with, and they were hurried off to their
last resting-place with scant ceremony and as little
delay as possible. Thus, what he saw was this: On a
low four-wheeled open cart or truck lay a coffin, a
black cloth carelessly flung over it, reeking with the
acrid odour of disinfectants. The cart was drawn by
a mule, with a man walking alongside as far from
the conveyance as the full length of the reins would
permit. At a distance of about fifteen yards behind
the improvised hearse, two or three relatives were
following at a brisk pace, palpably anxious to get
their painful duty over as quickly as possible.

A few minutes' walk brought George up to the

main entrance of the Hospital della Maddalena. He was greeted almost immediately upon his arrival by Father Vincent, who took him upstairs in a sort of parlour or anteroom. The monk's outward appearance was scarcely altered, though there was a briskness and alacrity about his voice and manner that seemed strange to George.

"I do not thank you for coming," were the monk's first words; "for I feel I have but Providence to thank. Of the motives that led you to this decision I know nothing; but now that you are here, I feel sure it is with a desire to work; and work there is, enough and to spare. We are so much reduced in numbers that I have now an entire ward under my immediate superintendence. Of course you can have had but little experience, if any, in hospital work, so I should like you to remain with me for the present. You will soon get to know all our different duties. But I must tell you at once the work we have to do in-doors is comparatively the easiest; what tries us most severely is that so many of the sick refuse to leave their own miserable homes, and prefer to die in squalor and misery without any medical assistance. They say the doctors poison them, poor deluded creatures! And there they lie, spreading further and further the germs of infection! We have occasionally to drag them to the hospitals almost by main force."

The imperturbable expression on George's face soon reassured the friar.

"You will require a few hours' rest now," the

monk continued; "and this afternoon, if you are willing, we will go with one of the doctors of the municipality to one of the poorest and most cholera-stricken quarters, in what is called the Fondaci."

The scene that met George's eyes that afternoon was one he never forgot. He found himself led through a labyrinth of little streets into a reeking alley, into which no ray of sun could ever penetrate, shut in on either side by houses five to six stories high. Situated below the level of the sea when the tide was high, the most nauseous effluvia, finding no outlet through the choked drains, would permeate the street gutters, exhaling pestilential miasmata which no breath of fresh air ever came to disperse or purify. And in this atmosphere of pollution a dense population swarmed like bees in a hive, every square inch being appropriated by a poor, wretched, squalid race of troglodytes, who lived and multiplied and died more like wild beasts than human beings, upon a soil black and putrid from the slow decomposition of organic substances accumulated during successive generations.

Going from door to door within this hotbed of infection, inquiring into the number and nature of the cases in each dwelling, frequently received with jeers, threats and insults, George Mansfield saw a side of life that, like so many of us, he had previously ignored—human suffering in its hourly never-ceasing intensity.

What originally was not much more than the kind-heartedness so frequently found in a manly, healthy nature, gradually developed and became ennobled into a genuine, self-sacrificing love of his suffering fellow creatures. All he had gone through himself seemed almost to shrink into insignificance when compared with the scenes of human misery worthy of Dante's Inferno that incessantly struck his eye.

With manly determination he threw himself into his work; no task was too irksome or too repulsive for him, and every errand of mercy among the seething population in the subterranean grottoes, from which many a stout heart might quail, he volunteered for. The panic-stricken people in the poorer quarters of Naples at the Porto and Mercato soon began to know the "Frate Inglese," as he was called, and to look upon him as a friend. They appeared to have none of the distrust towards him that filled their hearts against their compatriots who came with the endeavour to relieve them.

His heart would grow soft towards these simple-minded people, going from one extreme to the other —from panic-stricken ferocity to child-like submission. Father Vincent watched the change that so short a space of time had wrought in George with intense interest, thankful in his heart that what he looked upon as little short of a miracle had thus been accomplished. He never questioned George as to the motives that had prompted him: but the two friends understood each other without many words being exchanged.

Weeks went round without any signs of the

epidemic relenting—weeks spent by George Mansfield in incessant toil in an atmosphere poisoned by miasmata and laden with the fumes of sulphur, huge bonfires of which were nightly lighted throughout the streets of Naples. The want of sleep and fresh air was beginning to tell even upon his robust constitution. There was a wan and haggard expression about his face, and the deep black marks that encircled his eyes told an eloquent tale. As time went on his name became a household word amongst the poorer classes in the slums of the city. Many looked upon him almost as a saint, and a marvellous immunity from infection which he apparently possessed confirmed the popular belief. He had rapidly acquired a smattering of the quaint Neapolitan patois, which enabled him to be more independent of Father Vincent's direction; and he was thus enabled to go off unassisted on his errands of mercy. Wherever help was most urgently required George was always to be found; and even the authorities, though constitutionally intolerant of any unofficial assistance, presented him with a testimonial.

As the cooler weather set in and a diminution in the spread of the disease became perceptible, Father Vincent one day took George aside and spoke to him earnestly and pressingly about the imperative necessity of granting himself a few week's rest and change of scenery. "The pupil has far outdone the master," he said, with his quiet, sad smile; "and I have now more to learn from you than you ever could from me. But, say yourself, are you not far happier now than you were in days when"—he faltered in search of a suitable expression—"your face used to bear that restless, careworn expression?"

George burst out laughing: "I am sure I don't know much about the expression of my face, but I see what you mean. Was I happier then or now? Who can tell? What makes me happy now would not have done so then, and *vice versâ*. But as to my health, don't worry yourself about that. I have got a touch of fever; but otherwise I am all right, and there is plenty of work left for me to do. Let me be useful as long as I can—you see I have so many years to make up for." And then he confided to the monk that one of his patients, a poor fisherman's wife from the Mercato, who for many weary days was hovering between life and death, had now gone to join her poor husband, and before departing, had confided to his care her little curly-haired, dark-eyed girl, aged five, and that he had not dared refuse the prayer of the dying woman.

After some conversation between them, it was decided that the child, who already loved George for the devotion he had shown her parents, should be placed in a convent in the neighbourhood of Rome. As soon as George felt his work at Naples was at an end, he proposed spending a few weeks at or near Rome, to make the necessary arrangements. In order to be in the more immediate vicinity of his charge, he accepted Father Vincent's offer to give him letters for the father superior of the monastery of the Tre Fontane, situated close to the convent where the child, whose charge he had accepted, was to be brought up.

There was nothing that savoured of bigotry or narrow-mindedness in Father Vincent's religious views; and, though he made no secret of his earnest longing for George to join the Church to which he himself belonged, he never fell into the error of injudicious proselytism. Scant time was left George for religious meditations; still he had grown too familiar with the beautiful rites of the Catholic Church, which he saw performed daily at more than one bedside, not to feel at times powerfully drawn towards a faith which, even its opponents would hardly gainsay, is maligned the most vehemently by those who are most ignorant of it. Anyhow, no resolution had at that time ripened in George's mind on the subject.

CHAPTER XXI.

"Come, gentle Death, the ebbe of care,
   The ebbe of care, the flood of life;
The flood of life, the joyful fare;
   The joyful fare, the end of strife;
The end of strife: that thing wish I:
   Wherefore come, Death, and let me die!"
                    SIR THOMAS WYATT.

THERE is scarcely a more weird and desolate-
looking spot in the vast expanse of the Roman Campagna than the Tre Fontane. Nature has baffled the
many attempts made by successive generations at
draining, cultivating and making permanently inhabitable a spot which she had marked out to be a desert
and a wilderness, shrouded in the dense vapours that
rise at sunset from the marshy soil. Extensive plan-
tations of eucalyptus, and drainage works carried on
almost incessantly by convicts in their picturesque
scarlet prison garb, have no doubt done something
latterly to improve the sanitary conditions in the
neighbourhood; nevertheless, the mortality is great
amongst the poor Trappist monks who have settled
there, as if anxious to reduce the span of time that
separates them from the transition to eternal bliss.
Pale and hollow-faced, they flit about more like spirits
than like beings not yet free from all the weaknesses

and wants of human nature; nursing each other in turn as the malaria scourge fixes first upon one and then upon the other amongst them, but chiefly attentive to the requirements of the scanty and indigent population of *contadini* that, under the broiling midday sun, endeavour to extract a wretched livelihood from the cultivation of a well-nigh barren soil. To these poor *frati* the field labourers will look for assistance when, stricken down by the malarial fever, they have to return to their miserable little huts; and, with never a word of complaint, day after day the weary circuit is commenced by these humble apostles of privation and self-abnegation, dispensing, as much as their poor means will allow, food, medicine and spiritual consolation.

But hark! Amongst these weird surroundings, was not that the sound of the horn faintly discernible just beyond the brow of the hill, and surely the cheery notes of "Warrior! here, Warrior!" are from the lips of Harry Reynolds, the jovial huntsman of the Roman Foxhounds. Leisurely, at a slow jog trot, he is bringing his pack to the meet at the Tre Fontane, the desolate surroundings of which will for a short time be awakened from their slumbers. Already the refreshment tent that forms a prominent feature in all the meets in the Roman Campagna has been erected; grooms and second horsemen are appearing on the scene in rapid succession, and a long string of carriages is conveying the members of the Hunt to the *appuntamento*.

The field is no doubt a small one, if we apply to

it the standard of Kirby Gate or Badminton Park; but, if numerically weak, there is certainly no lack of quality, either in the stamp of hunters that are being led around, or in the men and women gradually collecting under the tent. And with what undeniable pluck and judgment many of them will ride over a country intersected, at rare intervals it is true, by those most formidable impediments to rapid progress known as *staccionate*, which will at first puzzle the boldest and cleverest timber-jumper! With a look of intense interest and curiosity in their emaciated faces the Trappist monks are looking on, just outside the gates that lead to the gardens of the monastery. In Italy, and more especially in Rome, the monk is, as a rule, rather a popular personage, and is always sure of meeting with a hearty reception whenever he emerges from his cell. Though, of course, debarred by the rules of their Order from all but the most transitory and fugitive intercourse with the outer world, there is none of that unsurpassable barrier that in most countries separates the monk from the layman. A strange contrast it no doubt is to see the burly figure of the whip, who has left his father's little farm in Yorkshire so many years ago that the Italian has grown to him almost as familiar as his own native tongue, bending over his horse's neck in earnest conversation with a sallow-faced monk in his rough brown cowl. And yet, strange though it may seem, there is a common topic of interest between the two; for the monks of the Tre Fontane have for some years back been entrusted with the walking of

a couple or two of hound puppies on their extensive
grounds with remarkable success.

A slight breeze, that tempers the heat of the sun
pouring down from a cloudless sky, is slowly rising,
swaying the long grass on the slopes beyond to and
fro, and rustling amongst the grey leaves of the
eucalyptus trees. Far in the distance the dome of
St. Peter's stands out boldly against the horizon, and
in the foreground the eye is attracted by the huge
white pile of the Basilica of S. Paolo fuori le Mura.
It is in that direction where lies the only road connecting the Tre Fontane with the City, that the eye
of the Roman M. F. H. is riveted. Repeatedly he
has pulled out his watch; and at last he is heard
muttering, half to himself and half to a friend standing within hearing: "How late Lady Devereux is
this morning! And yet I should like to give her
another few minutes' law, as we are almost sure to
find the moment we move off. What can have detained her?"

But before the words were uttered the look of
expectation on the manly, weatherbeaten face of the
speaker disappeared; for his sharp eye had caught
sight of the familiar outline of a phaeton spinning
along over the ruts and stones of the Roman high-
road, and rapidly approaching the meet.

"Am I very late, Duke?" said Lady Devereux, as
she alighted. "It was too kind of you, waiting for me;
but my husband was not very well this morning; so
that rather detained me. But don't trouble any more
about me; I shall overtake you in no time."

No matter how hardy the constitution may be, Nature will revenge herself, sooner or later, for any liberties taken with her laws; and thus, acting upon the stern commands of his medical advisers, Lord Devereux had decided during the autumn of 188 — to tear himself away from home comforts, sporting and other pastimes, and to winter in the Sunny South. Once he was obliged to go abroad, it mattered little to him what his destination was, and he willingly acquiesced in Mildred's suggestion of taking an apartment in Rome for the winter. The report of George's acts of devotion and downright heroism in the cholera hospitals of Naples had sent a thrill through the innermost depths of her nature and had thrown a halo of romance around him. She felt at last that all her early expectations concerning him had been verified, and that the idol she had worshipped was not — as at one time she had feared—simply common clay. The numerous letters of introduction she brought with her speedily enabled her to make friends amongst the essentially hospitable Roman society, where English visitors—once their credentials have been found to pass muster—are always sure of finding the most hearty welcome; and plenty of mounts were always placed at her disposal whenever she felt inclined for a gallop with the Roman Fox-hounds.

Lord Devereux's hunting days were pretty nearly over, but he would come out now and then, mounted on a sturdy cob, chiefly with a view to basking in the sun and talking to the ladies, whilst watching with a somewhat critical eye the general proceedings around him. The months that had gone by had not appreciably altered Lady Devereux's personal appearance, though her manner had perhaps grown slightly more absent, as if all that passed around her was barely perceived, and left no impression on a mind rising further and further above the little trivialities of every-day life.

As the hounds are seen moving off, she nimbly alights from her phaeton, assisted by Don Giovanni Barozzi—a light-hearted, lady-killing Roman prince, who had offered her a mount on a big, slashing bay, warranted safe over any kind of timber, and with a rare turn of speed over the top of the ground. Though in every respect worthy of his patronymic of Don Giovanni, he was too keen a sportsman to waste time on pretty speeches when hounds are just on the move; so, after a very short greeting, he placed Mildred in the saddle. Whilst he was arranging the folds of her skirt, one of the monks, who had been a silent observer of the scene, was noticed to approach him with a bashful look upon his face, as if doubting his own ability to acquit himself of the errand entrusted to him. Nevertheless, he summoned up sufficient courage, and almost in a whisper, said a few words to Prince Barozzi in his own language. The latter only shrugged his shoulders with rather a curt reply, and was about to move on, when Mildred quite accidentally asked him what the confidential communication just imparted by the monk had been. "It must be something very important," she added with a smile, "or I suppose my presence would have kept him at a respectful distance."

"Do you really want to know?" said Prince Barozzi, slightly raising his eyebrows. "Well, what he told me is this. There is a poor fellow, an Englishman, dying there from low fever; he is not actually a monk at present, it seems: he only came up a few days ago after having worked in the cholera hospitals at Naples, and has now caught malaria. He is not very fluent in Italian, and the monk thought that if some countryman of his happened to be present it might help the poor fellow in his last moments. I told him they had all gone on, and that there was nobody left here but you and me."

Mildred's cheek had grown as white as marble. "I think I ought to go and see the poor man," she said. "Will you ask what his name is?"

Somewhat reluctantly, the request was acquiesced in. "I can't quite make out the name: I make it to be something like Manffy, or Manfell."

"Don't trouble about me, Prince; I will come on later. Whoever this man is, I cannot let him die here all alone, with nobody who can even understand his last words. No, it would be no good your staying with me; I really would sooner you did not; and your groom can look after the mare whilst I go in." And without waiting for an answer, she slipped off her saddle on to the ground.

A look of puzzled uncertainty lingered on Don

Giovanni's handsome face. To be sure, how eccentric these English people always were! "Anyhow," he said, "before you decide upon staying, let me find out if they will allow you inside the monastery. I should think most likely they won't;" and he addressed a few words in Italian to the monk who was standing close by, anxiously awaiting a reply. "Yes;" he turned to her once more; "he says you can go in, for the man is not in Holy Orders as yet, and he is in the infirmary, not in the monastery itself. But are you quite sure you ought to go in? If you are determined to do so, and would prefer my not remaining, of course I will do as you wish. I will leave my second horseman here, and he will help you to find the hounds again when you come on later. They are not going very far just now, for they have heard of an outlying fox near those ruins over there." And lifting his hat, he trotted off in the wake of the gradually disappearing horsemen.

For a few seconds after his departure, Lady Devereux stood almost motionless. A voice within her told her that her next few steps would bring her face to face with the man, now on his deathbed, who had moulded her life's destiny. Her courage, she well knew, was not likely to fail her; but she was anxious to devise some means of avoiding anything like a shock which her sudden entrance might cause to the dying man. Not without some difficulty she made the monk who accompanied her understand her wish that he should precede her to the sick-room and say that a countrywoman of the

patient had come to inquire whether she could offer
him any assistance. "And say," she added, "that
perhaps it may be an old friend of his, but that
you do not know for certain."

Very few seconds afterwards she was in the sick-
room alone with George Mansfield. The blinds were
drawn to ward off the rays of the sun that were
beating down on the solitary window of the little
cell. With his face turned away from the light, the
sick man lay on a narrow little bed of most primitive
construction. The scanty furniture was of claustral
simplicity and austerity. But if his surroundings
were mean and humble—those of the veriest pauper,
in fact—there was no look of want or discontent
upon the pale, emaciated features that bore the
stamp of sublime resignation transfigured by suffering and awaiting rather than dreading a speedy
end.

A feverish flush rose to his cheeks as he turned
his head towards the door that admitted Lady Devereux. The look of tranquil composure upon his
face was intensified and lighted up by a pale smile,
but no trace of surprise was noticeable. His thoughts
had perhaps been wandering back to olden days—
the limits of time and distance vanish from the mind
as it looks onward and upward before taking leave
of this finite life of ours—and it seemed but natural
that she from whom he had been mentally taking
leave should now appear before him. Noiselessly
Lady Devereux slipped into the room; she put her
finger to her lips as if to impose silence upon him.

"I heard you were lying ill here; so I have come to look after you. But you must not get feverish or restless at my taking you by surprise in this manner. I mean to come back very often, or rather I should like to see you moved away to some healthier spot."

He clasped the hand that was proffered him. "It must, indeed, have been Providence that sent you here to light my last few hours. No; you must not think of moving me, or anything of the kind. Believe me, it is not worth while." And a faint smile flitted across his lips. He would not listen to her remonstrance, and went on: "You must not pity me, either; for, believe me, I am not unhappy at the idea of dying—much less so now that I am able to see you once more before all is over. There is so much that I have to tell you, so much that I could hardly tell you when full of life and strength. But the last words of a dying man can compromise nobody, can they? I am afraid I have wronged and injured you throughout your whole life—unintentionally, God knows; but still I have done so. I know you are not happy—that all your noblest gifts are thrown away and wasted; and often I have felt I was the cause of much of this."

"I will not let you say that, George," she gently interrupted. "My life at times has been a little arduous; but all that is nearly over now. But don't let us waste these precious moments talking about me; I want to know all about yourself all in your past life that I do not yet know. I would like to hear it from your own lips; and, although I cannot for a moment believe you are as ill as you say—tell me, is there anything that you would wish me to do? Any message, whatever it may be, shall be carried out."

"I wonder what the poor old monks outside will think," said George, with the bright look of olden days returning once more, though only for a few seconds, "when they hear of my deathbed confession being made to a lovely vision, in the smartest of riding habits? But, no matter!" And after a few moments' reflection: "No; I don't think I have any very special message for anyone. Of course, you will say something to Errington; but I am afraid I shall not leave any great blank with anybody. Just let me have a drop out of that cup; I feel so terribly weak again. There, that is better. And now, Mildred, before we part for ever, let me once more thank you for all you have been, and all you would have been to me, had an evil Fate not kept us apart. Your influence would have ennobled and sanctified my whole poor life. It was not to be; but I want you not to think too harshly of the woman who turned aside the current of my destiny. Everything appears so different when you are on the point of taking leave of this world; and I can now look back dispassionately upon that stormy period of my life. But when I do so, I really think these last six months have been my happiest time. One look of gratitude I saw in the tearful, dark eyes of a poor Neapolitan fisherman's wife, when I told her that her little girl, whom we were attend-

ing to, was likely to recover, gave me far more intense
happiness than any other moment in my life that I
can think of. I should like to hear you say before
it is too late that you forgive me all the wrong I
have done you, wittingly or unwittingly. When I
went out to Hungary, or rather soon after I got there,
the thought of your marrying another seemed to
haunt me day and night. That is how it all began.
And now, I know you would not wish me yourself in
my dying hour to trample upon what I have worshipped. I will only say one word more about her.
Whatever you may have heard, beware what you believe! She had been sinned against more than she
had sinned, and her mind was pure and noble in
spite of all the temptations that beset her at every
step through life. How distant it all seems," he
added, his voice getting weaker and weaker. "But,
Mildred, can you say you forgive me? I should die
happier if I just heard that one word."

"Forgive you, darling!" Mildred answered in the
softest tones, close to the dying man's ear; "Have
I anything to forgive? Why go back to sad times
long past? Let us rather be thankful that we have
once more been brought together. Of course I did
suffer when I heard how soon and how completely I
was forgotten, and that a few hours, so to speak,
sufficed to wipe out the memory of years. How
little you must know me really to have supposed
that I could have married another had it not been
that I saw no other way of saving *you*. How strange
that you should not have guessed that!"

A deep tremor of emotion passed over the features about which the shadow of Death was hovering, and he answered, in a voice barely audible: "So you have sacrificed yourself for me!"

"Don't say that, darling," she interrupted him. "I am quite happy, in a way, and anyhow the worst is over now. I have felt so happy thinking of you all these last months—so proud of you."

"There is, indeed, nothing to be proud of: dozens of others did as much, and more. At least, now that all is over, I may say that I die in peace and goodwill with all men, and with the thought that my life has not been altogether wasted. Mildred, will you do one last thing for me? That little Neapolitan girl I was just telling you of—a sweet, dark-eyed little thing, about five years old; Biba, they call it—is at the convent on the Monte Oliveto near here. Both of her parents died of cholera, and I promised her mother that I would look after the child. May I now transfer the trust upon you?"

"Of course, I will take care of her as if she was my own. But hark! what is that?"

Roman foxes are not, as a rule, straight-necked; their line is mostly a circuitous one, such as we are accustomed to with harriers. Scent proved bad on this particular morning, and much delay occurred before a fox was found basking in the sun in an osier-bed within only a short distance from the meet. After a slow hunting run, Reynard was bearing back to his old quarters, and the shrill note of the huntsman's "Forrard, forrard away!" was plainly audible in the room where George Mansfield was slowly breathing his last.

His mind began to wander; the familiar sound brought back recollections of days long gone by, and visions of different phases of his life followed each other in rapid succession across his feverish mind. But life's candle was burnt out, and the last flickering of it only foreboded the rapid end. In a voice hardly audible, and drawing Mildred closer against him, he said: "Mildred, let my last words be a blessing to you. I have lived and loved, and my life has been one of self-indulgence and of sin; but no one knows what I have suffered. I can now say I die happily. Say once more you have forgiven me."

These were his last words; for, with a short gasp, his head fell back upon the pillow.

Within hardly more than a stone's throw from the monastery a gallant old dog-fox had bravely met his death, and the merry chatter of horsemen discussing the various episodes of the run, was filling the deserted neighbourhood. With a look of surprise and anxiety upon his handsome face, Don Giovanni trotted up to the Tre Fontane and inquired from his second horseman whether Lady Devereux had returned to town. On being answered in the negative, he rapidly dismounted and walked up to the infirmary.

A corpse lay on the little narrow bed, and kneeling by it was the figure of a woman, sobbing and praying the Angel of Death once more to stretch out his wand and to unite within his cold grasp what a Life's Destiny had kept asunder.

THE END.